# Demystifying AI through Due Diligence and Data Management

— A GOVERNANCE GUIDE —

Catherine Barrett

AMERICAN BAR ASSOCIATION
Science & Technology Law Section

Cover design by Amanda Fry/ABA Design



Printed in the United States of America.

29 28 27 26 25 5 4 3 2 1

A catalog record for this book is available from the Library of Congress.

# Contents

# Acknowledgments

I dedicate this book to all the dear friends, colleagues, and mentors who have supported me personally and professionally over the years, including my husband Mike for his patience and endless humor; my brilliant and insightful former colleagues at MITRE, including Barbara, Emily, Holly, Liz, Nancy, and many others; and Sarah Swank for her inspired leadership in the field of healthcare AI.

A special thanks also to Michael Aisenburg, Sarah Orwig, and the leadership of the American Bar Association for the many opportunities to publish articles on science, technology, and the law.

Finally, and most of all, I dedicate this book to my loving son Connor, who I am sure will one day be a caring and compassionate leader among the future generations of humans who will help ensure we witness many profound societal benefits from AI while limiting its potential perils.

# About the Author

Catherine Barrett is founder and CEO of Annapolis Analytics, Inc., a consulting firm specializing in AI governance and data management, cybersecurity risk management, and data privacy and security matters. Ms. Barrett, formerly with the MITRE Corporation as a Principal Cyber Policy consultant, was vice-chair of the Information Security Committee of the Science and Technology Law Section of the American Bar Association (ABA) for the 2019–2022 period. Previously, she was vice-chair of the ABA public health and policy interest group for the 2014–2015 period. She is also coauthor of *What Is Telemedicine?*, published by the ABA in 2015.

At MITRE, Ms. Barrett provided federal clients in the health, intelligence, and defense communities with research, analysis, and counsel regarding federal and state data privacy and security laws as well as federal cybersecurity laws and policies. Prior to joining MITRE, Ms. Barrett worked as a consultant for Booz Allen Hamilton (McLean, VA) and Booz & Company (Sydney, Australia), where she provided consulting services to private- and public-sector clients. She is also a former healthcare lobbyist and U.S. Senate staffer.

Ms. Barrett, along with fellow ABA members, served as a panelist at the 2020 and 2021 RSA Conferences, where she gave presentations on state laws governing data brokers and the role of contractual due diligence in shoring up supply chain security, respectively.

Ms. Barrett received her JD and MBA from American University Washington College of Law and Kogod School of Business, respectively. In 2022, she completed an MS in information and communications technology with a concentration in information systems security from the University of Denver and holds a Systems Security Certified Practitioner (SSCP) certificate.

Ms. Barrett graduated cum laude from Regis University with a BA in political science and BS in economics.

Ms. Barrett's professional memberships include the ABA, the International Information System Security Certification Consortium (ISC2), and the International Association of Privacy Professionals (IAPP).

Ms. Barrett and her husband have one son and reside in Dublin, Ireland.

*"The arc of the moral universe is long, but it bends toward the algorithm."*

—Ian Bremmer, founder and president of
Eurasia Group (November 6, 2024)

# Executive Summary

Regardless of how you feel about the prominence of artificial intelligence (AI) in the world today—whether it is a revolutionary technology on par with the invention and uptake of electricity, or not—academia, private-sector firms, and governments are investing billions in AI. The scale and speed of AI innovations have surprised thought leaders such as Dr. Geoffrey Hinton, "Godfather of AI," former advisor to Google, and the winner of the 2024 Nobel Prize in Physics, who admits, "I didn't think we'd get here in only 40 years."[1] In addition to the unexpected scale and speed of AI innovation, the risk that AI could be used for nefarious purposes is worrisome to AI thought leaders such as former Google CEO Eric Schmidt, who argues AI in the wrong hands could lead to existential threats to mankind.[2] For example, rogue nation-states such as North Korea or Iran could use AI technologies to accelerate the development of nuclear, chemical, and/or biological weapons. These ongoing trends in AI innovation—the scale, speed, and associated

1. Lance Ulanoff, "The Godfather of AI Is More Worried Than Ever About the Future of AI," techradar.com, April 28, 2025, https://www.techradar.com/computing/artificial-intelligence/the-godfather-of-ai-is-more-worried-than-ever-about-the-future-of-ai.

2. Imran Rahman-Jones, "Ex-Google Boss Fears for AI 'Bin Laden Scenario,'" *BBC News*, February 13, 2025, https://www.bbc.com/news/articles/c5y6eq2zxlno (last visited March 24, 2025).

risks—are noteworthy, as is the struggle to wrestle with the legal and regulatory implications of governing AI.

While the debate about revolutionary or not carries on, understanding AI, particularly the underlying algorithms, data, models, and the associated risk, is important to all of us. AI is here to stay and is being woven into the fabric of our lives, often without notice and/or user consent. Microsoft Outlook, Meta WhatsApp, Google Search, and Apple iPhone integrate AI into the latest software updates and do not appear to provide an option to decline AI in the applications.[3] What data are being collected, organized, used, transferred, and so on from the updated versions of these and other AI-enhanced applications? Do we want notice and the ability to decline AI-enhanced applications as a society? Do we care? How are data harvested using AI collected, organized, used, and stored? What other questions do we need to ask of AI developers, vendors, and others about the role of this technology in society, including our lives?

This book is for anyone curious to know more about the role algorithms—the "black box"—play in AI and the importance of governing algorithms, data, and AI within an organization. It offers a practical approach to understanding and managing possible risks associated with algorithms and AI. It includes aids such as policy templates and a checklist to help manage AI within organizations. While the book focuses on algorithmic governance, a subset of AI governance, this book does not delve into the mathematical underpinnings of algorithms, AI models, or coding languages used to develop AI-related technologies. Rather, this book invites a higher-level understanding of these concepts without requiring a technical background.

The audience for this book includes lawyers, consultants, entrepreneurs, business leaders, and others who are looking to understand what questions to ask to identify and manage risks associated with AI technologies, including applications.

---

3. Apple, "How to Get Apple Intelligence," January 30, 2025, https://support.apple.com/en-ie/121115 (last visited March 24, 2025).

The questions were developed from researching publications of leading academic institutions such as MIT and Stanford; books written by legal scholars and mathematicians; nonprofit organizations focused on information security and AI; and private-sector technology companies such as IBM, OpenAI, Meta, and Google, among others. The appendices include various AI policy templates that may be tailored to suit individual needs.

## What Is Artificial Intelligence?

The definition of AI varies, but generally, the term refers to "the science of making machines do things that would require intelligence if done by man."[4] These "things" include human reasoning, decision-making, planning, communicating, and predicting, among others.[5] In 2018, Congress formally defined AI in Section 238(g) of the National Defense Authorization Act of 2019 (Public Law 115-232) (Figure 1). Subsequently, this definition was referenced in Executive Order 13960, "Promoting the Use of Trustworthy Artificial Intelligence in the Federal Government" (December 3, 2020).

Although there may not be one agreed-upon, standard definition of AI, the emerging common theme is that machines take on characteristics normally associated with humans, such as thinking, learning, drawing inferences, and acting rationally.

4. B. Custers & E. Fosch-Villaronga (eds.), *Law and Artificial Intelligence: Regulating AI and Applying AI in Legal Practice*, p. 44, T.M.C. Asser Press (2022).

5. National Aeronautics and Space Administration, "What Is Artificial Intelligence?," May 13, 2024, https://www.nasa.gov/what-is-artificial-intelligence/ (last visited March 17, 2025).

AI includes:

1. Any artificial system that performs tasks under varying and unpredictable circumstances without significant human oversight, or that can learn from experience and improve performance when exposed to data sets.
2. An artificial system developed in computer software, physical hardware, or other context that solves tasks requiring human-like perception, cognition, planning, learning, communication, or physical action.
3. An artificial system designed to think or act like a human, including cognitive architectures and neural networks.
4. A set of techniques, including machine learning, that is designed to approximate a cognitive task.
5. An artificial system designed to act rationally, including an intelligent software agent or embodied robot that achieves goals using perception, planning, reasoning, learning, communicating, decision making, and acting.

**Figure 1: Definition of Artificial Intelligence, Section 238(g) of the National Defense Authorization Act of 2019**

## AI Is Inherently Complex

AI is complex because of the vast quantities of data used to train AI models, the breadth and depth of software code used to create AI, "and the incomprehensible nature of the inner workings of algorithms."[6] Computer science professionals and mathematicians may understand AI algorithms, data sets, and models, but not all of us have or can access that level of expertise. This book is intended to be a reference for practitioners who need to know what questions to ask and what policies need to be in place to manage AI, not the intricate, technical details of how AI technologies work. Although there is a lot of hype around AI, it's important to remember it's not magic; it's math.

6. Daron Acemoglu, "Harms of AI," in Justin B. Bullock et al. (eds.), *The Oxford Handbook of AI Governance*, p. 480, Oxford University Press (2024).

## AI Is Evolving Rapidly

AI is rapidly evolving with ever-increasing commercial applications across the economy, but practitioners may not be aware of the potential risks associated with AI technologies. For example, when the Chinese open-source AI assistant DeepSeek debuted in January 2025, millions downloaded the application to their electronic devices and began experimenting with the platform. Much like ChatGPT, Claude, Google Gemini, Microsoft Copilot, and Perplexity AI, DeepSeek is free to download and use (as of June 2025) and provides advanced search functions to identify and "review literature, spot research gaps, and access special resources."[7] However, unsuspecting users may not realize the data privacy and/or security risks associated with downloading and using DeepSeek.

According to the privacy policy, for example, DeepSeek automatically collects personal data when using the application, including "your device model, operating system, IP address, device identifiers and system language . . . features you use and the actions you take . . . [and] your approximate location based on IP address . . ."[8] Furthermore, personal data may be collected, processed, and stored in the People's Republic of China. As this example illustrates, due diligence of AI technologies is necessary to identify, understand, and manage associated risks prior to introducing AI into an environment.

This book provides an overview of many AI-related risks as well as risk mitigation measures. Policy templates included in the appendices provide a practical approach to managing AI-related risks to benefit clients and organizations.

---

7. DeepSeek AI Team, "What Is DeepSeek," DeepSeek.com, March 22, 2025, https://deepseek.ai/blog/what-is-deep-seek (last visited June 3, 2025).

8. DeepSeek, "DeepSeek Privacy Policy," April 28, 2025, https://cdn.deepseek.com/policies/en-US/deepseek-privacy-policy.html (last visited June 3, 2025).

## AI Isn't Powered by Magic; It's Powered by Math

Algorithms power AI technologies. Often referred to as the "black box" in AI, algorithms use mathematical concepts such as statistics, calculus, abstract algebra, and number theory, among others, to create complex sets of instructions for computers to follow to achieve a defined objective.[9] An algorithm is "any well-defined computational procedure that takes some value, or set of values, as input and produces some value, or set of values, as output" in a defined period of time.[10] Algorithms process data via automated systems such as AI applications, which, in turn, power machine learning (ML) techniques.[11] ML is "a subfield of AI involving algorithms that enable computer systems to iteratively learn from and then make decisions, inferences, or predictions based on input data."[12]

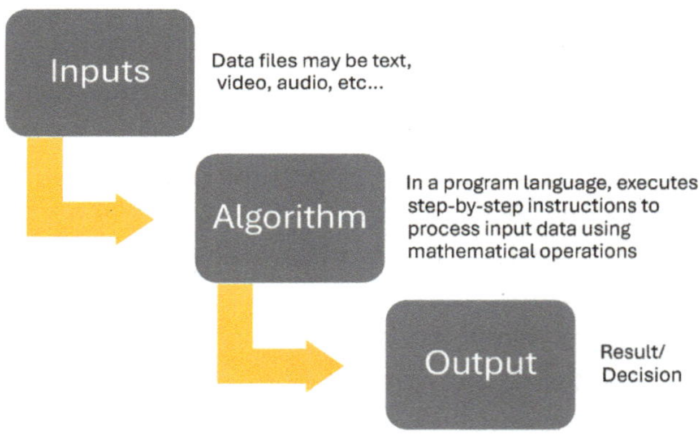


9. Thomas H. Cormen, Charles E. Leiserson, Ronald L. Rivest & Clifford Stein, *Introduction to Algorithms*, 4th ed., p. xiii, The MIT Press: Cambridge, Massachusetts (2022).

10. *Id.*

11. The UK Digital Regulation Cooperation Forum, "Research and Analysis: The Benefits and Harms of Algorithms: A Shared Perspective from the Four Digital Regulators," September 23, 2022, https://www.gov.uk/government/publications/findings-from-the-drcf-algorithmic-processing-workstream-spring-2022/the-benefits-and-harms-of-algorithms-a-shared-perspective-from-the-four-digital-regulators (last visited March 8, 2025).

12. IAPP, "Key Terms for AI Governance," July 2024, https://iapp.org/resources/article/key-terms-for-ai-governance/ (last visited March 31, 2025).

ML trains computers to learn from experience rather than following a predetermined equation, to process data using computational methods that "learn" information directly from data.[13] ML enables computers to imitate how "humans learn, to perform tasks autonomously, and to improve their performance and accuracy through experience and exposure to more data."[14]

Although advanced math and computer program language may be used to create algorithms, the underlying concept is very relatable and basic. If you've ever followed a recipe or performed activities of daily living such as getting washed and dressed in the morning, you've followed an algorithm—a set of instructions—to accomplish a specific output or goal, whether to make a meal or start your morning to get off to work or school, for example. Algorithms use sophisticated math and computer language so computers can understand the instructions to accomplish tasks/goals. But, like a set of instructions used to create a recipe, algorithms are just mathematical instructions a computer uses to solve a problem or perform a task. It's just math, not magic.

13. The UK Digital Regulation Cooperation Forum, "Research and Analysis: The Benefits and Harms of Algorithms: A Shared Perspective from the Four Digital Regulators," September 23, 2022, https://www.gov.uk/government/publications/findings-from-the-drcf-algorithmic-processing-workstream-spring-2022/the-benefits-and-harms-of-algorithms-a-shared-perspective-from-the-four-digital-regulators (last visited March 8, 2025).

14. IBM, "What Is Machine Learning?," https://www.ibm.com/think/topics/machine-learning (last visited March 9, 2025).

*"Every AI system is necessarily a reflection of the data on which it is trained."*

—Christopher S. Yoo (2024)[15]

15. Christopher S. Yoo, "Beyond Algorithmic Disclosure for AI," 25 *Colum. Sci. & Tech. L. Rev.* 314 (2024).

# II

# Introduction

Do apocalyptic predictions about AI keep you up at night? Do you worry AI will take over human decision-making and launch weapons of mass destruction, conventional and/or cyberspace, thereby ending human civilization? Do you worry AI will lead to an inability for humans to distinguish between misinformation and fact, thereby leading to the downfall of information-based economies and governments? While some may sound the alarm, others in research and academia caution against these doomsday scenarios. Many believe sensationalizing AI distracts from more immediate, practical issues such as AI governance and risk management.

AI is here to stay and is already impacting society across all sectors of the economy. For example, some of the more promising applications of AI are in the healthcare sector, specifically in pharmaceutical drug discovery, disease diagnosis, patient monitoring, and natural language processing and data analytics "to extract value-adding outcomes from medical literature and pathology reports."[16] Natural language processing is "a subfield of AI that helps computers understand, interpret and manipulate human language by transforming information into

16. Massachusetts Institute of Technology, Management Executive Education in Artificial Intelligence in Health Care, "Course Curriculum," https://executive.mit.edu/course/artificial-intelligence-in-health-care/a056g00000URaaTAAT.html (last visited March 2, 2025).

content."[17] Lawyers are using AI to change how they practice, leveraging AI tools to draft legal memoranda, review contracts, and conduct legal research. Lawyers may use AI tools to complete more mundane tasks, thereby freeing up time to devote to more intellectually intensive tasks. While AI may be used in healthcare and law to augment work and increase efficiency, the technology industry is replacing human labor with AI tools. Software developers, help desk/tech support, data/business analysts, and overhead corporate roles in communications, legal, and marketing departments are being replaced by AI in technology and social media companies, for example.[18]

The more urgent, immediate need is to democratize AI, demystify AI technologies' inner workings, and understand potential risks. Due diligence requires looking under the hood and digging into the "black box" that powers AI—the algorithms. Just as law schools stress the importance of writing in plain English, innovators, researchers, and AI vendors should explain in plain English how algorithms operate, the significance of certain mathematical concepts used in algorithms (e.g., weights and variables), the source and scope of training data, and "disclosures about the way that the system was tested" to understand "the circumstances under which an algorithm is likely to perform well."[19]

This book sheds light on the "black box" to aid in conducting due diligence on AI products and services and provide practical AI governance and risk management advice and suggested templates. Regardless of how the legal and regulatory landscape evolves, this book provides practical steps to manage AI

---

17. IAPP, "Key Terms for AI Governance," July 2024, https://iapp.org/resources/article/key-terms-for-ai-governance/ (last visited March 31, 2025).

18. Jason Snyder, "AI Reset: Layoffs, RTO, and the New Realities of Work," *Forbes*, February 12, 2025, https://www.forbes.com/sites/jasonsnyder/2025/02/12/ai-reset-layoffs-rto-and-the-new-realities-of-work/ (last visited March 2, 2025).

19. Christopher S. Yoo, "Beyond Algorithmic Disclosure for AI," 25 *Colum. Sci. & Tech. L. Rev.* 314, 325 (2024).

technologies within an entity. It is a practical guide for lawyers, consultants, business leaders, and others interested in AI governance and risk management. AI will permeate every facet of our lives and future generations, so it is important to understand, interact with, assess, manage, and, if need be, decommission it.

*"[AI] is probably a more powerful weapon than the biggest weapons programs the U.S. sponsors."*

—Eric Schmidt, former CEO of Google (2024)[20]

20. Julie Bonette, "Eric Schmidt '76, Former Google CEO, Talks About the Future of AI," *Princeton Alumni Weekly*, November 22, 2024, https://paw.princeton.edu/article/eric-schmidt-76-former-google-ceo-talks-about-future-ai (last visited March 30, 2025).

III

# Background

The history of AI is peppered with innovations in mathematics and computer science. Stretching back more than two thousand years, scholars have tried to use "mathematical symbols and operations" to explain logic because, as George Boole (1815–1864) believed, "the human brain uses logic to think, so if we were to find a way to represent logic with mathematics, we would also have a mathematical description of how the brain works."[21] Thus, although AI may seem to have just recently entered the public consciousness, interest in the human brain and how it works is an ancient endeavor. Please see images on pages 16 and 17 to review key AI high-level milestones.

The term "AI" originated in the mid-1950s, when John McCarthy, a Dartmouth College professor, coined the phrase "artificial intelligence" to describe a workshop he organized "to clarify and develop ideas about thinking machines."[22] While Dartmouth gave birth to the name, Alan Turing—an English mathematician and "father of computer science"—gave birth to the idea of AI. In 1950, Turing published a groundbreaking paper, "Computing Machinery and Intelligence," in which he

21. Charles Petzold, "Logic with Switches," The Microsoft Press Store, October 25, 2022, https://www.microsoftpressstore.com/articles/printerfriendly/3150377 (last visited June 3, 2025).

22. Lawrence Livermore National Laboratory, "The Birth of Artificial Intelligence (AI) Research," https://st.llnl.gov/news/look-back/birth-artificial-intelligence-ai-research (last visited February 24, 2025).

posed the question, "Can machines think?"[23] Unlike Turing and McCarthy, Franklin Rosenblatt earned a PhD in psychology rather than mathematics. His contributions to AI can be traced back to 1958 when he developed the concept of "deep learning and neural networks, which can classify online images, for example, or enable language translation . . . ."[24] Deep learning is a subfield of AI and ML that uses artificial neural networks (ANN). Neural networks are a "type of model used in ML that mimics the way neurons in the brain interact with multiple processing layers, including at least one hidden layer."[25]

Generally, deep learning is applied where large volumes of raw data need to be processed, such as image recognition, neural language processing, and speech recognition.[26] In 1960, Stanford University engineer Dr. Bernard Widrow also focused on neural networks and human memory and is credited with inventing a single-layer ANN for pattern recognition, laying the foundation for future advances in neural networks and machine learning.[27]

Over the next couple of decades, a lull in funding for AI research and development slowed progress—a period referred to as the "AI Winter." Then, in 1997, the IBM Corporation stunned the world when its AI-enabled machine Deep Blue became "the first computer system in the world to defeat a reigning world chess champion . . . ."[28] Deep Blue's technology tackled complex calculations and uncovered database patterns, demonstrating for the first time "a future in which supercomputers and artificial intelligence could simulate human thinking."[29] Another key milestone in AI came in 2012 with the advent of AlexNet, "a deep learning neural network trained to recognize images of

23. *Id.*

24. Melanie Lefkowitz, "Professor's Perceptron Paved the Way for AI—60 Years Too Soon," *The Cornell Chronicle*, September 25, 2019, https://news.cornell.edu/stories/2019/09/professors-perceptron-paved-way-ai-60-years-too-soon (last visited February 25, 2025).

25. IAPP, "Key Terms for AI Governance," July 2024, https://iapp.org/resources/article/key-terms-for-ai-governance/ (last visited March 31, 2025).

26. *Id.*

27. https://www.nobelprize.org/uploads/2024/11/advanced-physicsprize2024-3.pdf.

28. IBM, "Deep Blue," https://www.ibm.com/history/deep-blue (last visited February 25, 2025).

29. *Id.*

objects such as dogs and cars" at a near-human level.[30] AlexNet was significant because of its "vast visual database designed for object recognition research" consisting of "over 14 million hand-annotated images with over 20,000 categories."[31]

The next leap forward in AI came in 2019 and 2020 with the release of OpenAI's Generative Pre-Trained Transformers 2 (GPT-2) and 3 (GPT-3), respectively. These conversational chatbots use natural language processing to answer queries on a seemingly endless array of topics. In addition, these GPTs may summarize text, draft legal memorandums, conduct research, generate ideas, and respond to instructions, for example. ChatGPT leverages large language models (LLMs) to train its models using reinforcement learning from human feedback (RLHF).[32] LLMs are a form of ML utilizing deep learning algorithms to create pretrained models on massive text data sets for the purpose of language learning to analyze and learn patterns and relationships among characters, words, and phrases.[33]

This refining process makes ChatGPT produce human-like language in a conversational style and allows users to use these AI applications with ease. While OpenAI's advanced chatbot captured the world's attention, researchers and academics, as well as government leaders throughout the world, are focused on investing in, regulating, and developing AI to advance economic and political objectives. It is well understood that the next AI frontier is artificial general intelligence (AGI)—a subset of AI that matches or surpasses human intelligence—and a race is on among countries from around the world to invent AGI, thereby capturing the economic and political powers that are sure to follow.

---

30. World Economic Forum, "A Short History of AI in 10 Landmark Moments," October 3, 2024, https://www.weforum.org/stories/2024/10/history-of-ai-artificial-intelligence/ (last visited February 24, 2025).

31. Nico Klingler, "AlexNet: A Revolutionary Deep Learning Architecture," Viso.ai, April 29, 2024, https://viso.ai/deep-learning/alexnet/ (last visited February 25, 2025).

32. Will Douglas Heaven, "The Inside Story of How ChatGPT Was Built from the People Who Made It," *MIT Technology Review*, March 3, 2023, https://www.technologyreview.com/2023/03/03/1069311/inside-story-oral-history-how-chatgpt-built-openai/ (last visited February 25, 2025).

33. IAPP, "Key Terms for AI Governance," July 2024, https://iapp.org/resources/article/key-terms-for-ai-governance/ (last visited March 31, 2025).

## Timeline of Key AI High-level Milestones (1/2)

**1950**

Alan Turing – the "father of computer science" – publishes a landmark paper: "Computing Machinery and Intelligence," wherein he poses the question: "Can Machines Think?"

**1954**

Dartmouth College mathematics Professor John McCarthy coined the phrase "artificial intelligence" to describe a research project exploring Dr. Alan Turing's query regarding whether machines can think.

**1958**

Dr. Franklin Rosenblatt, Cornell University, invents the perceptron, a "machine with a single-layer neural network capable of perceiving, recognizing and identifying its surroundings without any human training or control."

**1960**

Dr. Bernard Widrow, Standford University, invents a single-layer, artificial neural network for pattern recognition," laying "the foundation for future advances in neural networks and machine learning."

**1974–1980 & 1987–1994**

These periods of time are referred to as the "AI Winter," due to a lull in AI funding for research and development.

Alan Turing, National Security Agency/Central Security Service, https://www.nsa.gov/History/Cryptologic-History/Historical-Figures/Historical-Figures-View/Article/1621551/alan-turing/ (last visited February 24, 2025); Dartmouth College, "Artificial Intelligence Coined at Dartmouth," https://home.dartmouth.edu/about/artificial-intelligence-ai-coined-dartmouth (last visited June 25, 2025); Lefkowitz, Melanie, "Professor's perceptron paved the way for AI – 60 years too soon, *The Cornell Chronicle*, September 25, 2019, https://news.cornell.edu/stories/2019/09/professors-perceptron-paved-way-ai-60-years-too-soon (last visited February 25, 2025); Dr. Bernard Widrow, "Hall of Fame Members," Silicon Valley Engineering Council, 1999, https://www.svec.org/hall-of-fame-members/ (last visited February 24, 2025); National Oceanic & Atmospheric Administration, "Winter Weather," 2021, https://inside.nssl.noaa.gov/nsslnews/tag/winter-weather/ (last visited February 24, 2025).

## Timeline of Key AI High-level Milestones (2/2)

**1997**

IBM's "Deep Blue" became "the first computer system in the world to defeat a reigning world chess champion…" Deep Blue's technology tackled complex calculations and uncovered database patterns.

**2012**

AlexNet is the first example of a "deep learning neural network" and "marked a breakthrough in image recognition…[because it could] recognize images of objects such as dogs and cars at a level very close to humans."

**2019**

OpenAI's Generative Pre-trained Transformer 2 (GPT-2) is the most advanced chatbot to date and uses natural language processing to answer prompts from the public.

**2020**

OpenAI's GPT-3 catapulted the power of large language models (LLMs) into the wider public. GPT-3 provided human-like written text within seconds, was easy to use, and "introduced generative AI proper to the wider world."

**2021–present**

Competition among nations worldwide is growing to win the AI race for superiority in research, investment, innovation, financing, talent, and more. Winning the AI race means securing economic and political power.

IBM logo, https://www.ibm.com/brand/experience-guides/developer/brand/logo/?mhsrc=ibmsearch_a&mhq=IBM%20logo#ibm-8-bar-logo (last visited February 24, 2025); World Economic Forum, "A short history of AI in 10 landmark moments," World Economic Forum, October 3. 2024, https://www.weforum.org/stories/2024/10/history-of-ai-artificial-intelligence/ (last visited February 24, 2025); World Economic Forum, "A short history of AI in 10 landmark moments," World Economic Forum, October 3. 2024, https://www.weforum.org/stories/2024/10/history-of-ai-artificial-intelligence/ (last visited February 24, 2025); World Economic Forum, "A short history of AI in 10 landmark moments," World Economic Forum, October 3. 2024, https://www.weforum.org/stories/2024/10/history-of-ai-artificial-intelligence/ (last visited February 24, 2025); US Department of State, "Policy Issues: Science, Technology, and Innovation," https://www.state.gov/policy-issues/science-technology-and-innovation/ (last visited February 24, 2025).

*"We have the potential to dramatically improve our human condition in an AI-powered world, but . . . we need governance that is empirical, collaborative, and deeply rooted in human-centered values."*[34]

34. Fei-Fei Li, founding codirector of the Stanford Institute for Human-Centered AI (HAI) and CEO and cofounder of World Labs.

# IV

# The Importance of AI Governance and Risk Management

AI governance is an essential, foundational management practice comprised of policies, processes, people, and technology to identify, document, monitor, and mitigate risks associated with AI. AI governance also addresses the need for accountability, transparency, fairness, privacy, and security, among others (see Figure 2). Establishing AI governance and risk management infrastructure (people, processes, technologies) may face several challenges.[35]

First, AI is inherently complex, and there is a lack of AI expertise—technical skills and operational knowledge—to meet demand. Second, we face a lack of clear legal and regulatory guidance. Although some laws governing AI practices currently exist in the European Union (AI Act), there is no similar body of law in the United States, for example. Third, experts cannot fully explain some current AI innovations. Even AI developers sometimes cannot fully explain how an AI model works, for

35. Austin Chia & Chrissy Kidd, "AI Governance in 2025: A Full Perspective on Governance for Artificial Intelligence," Splunk.com, February 26, 2025, https://www.splunk.com/en_us/blog/learn/ai-governance.html (last visited March 31, 2025).

example.[36] While this list is not exhaustive, it does reflect some of the more prominent, enduring challenges to governing AI.

Overcoming these and other challenges to establish and operationalize AI governance within an organization is essential to manage risk. "AI-related risk factors include regulatory risks, operational risks, competitive risks, cybersecurity risks, ethical risks, and third-party risks," among others.[37] Lacking a comprehensive, organized approach to AI governance and associated risks threatens continuity of operations, raises potential legal liabilities, and creates other operational risks.

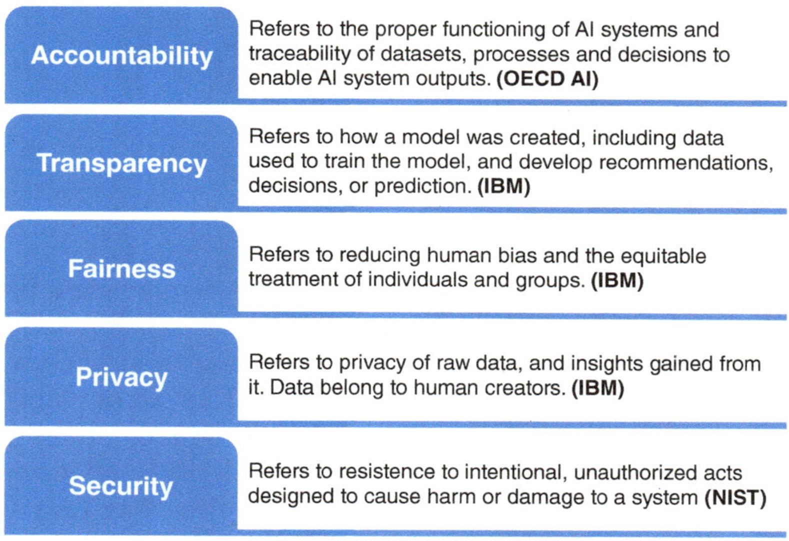


Figure 2: Key Components of AI Governance

There are at least four methods used to identify AI-related risks:

1. Algorithm Bias Audit (ABA)

   *Description:* Refers to a hypothesis-driven test whereby an AI system's inputs and outputs are evaluated to

---

36. *Id.*

37. Weil, Gotshal & Manges LLP, "Governance and Securities Alert," November 27, 2023, https://www.weil.com/-/media/mailings/2023/q4/sec-disclosures-of-artificial-intelligence-technologies-112723.pdf (last visited March 2, 2025).

determine whether AI outputs violate protected classes within society (e.g., discrimination based on sex, race, age, etc.).[38] These audits are typically performed on AI systems already in use and thus do not generally include an evaluation of the code. Instead, the ABA compares input data with AI output data. Input data is "data provided to or directly acquired by a learning algorithm or ML model" to produce an output.[39] For example, Pymetrics (now called Harver) hired an external team "of computer scientists from Northeastern University to audit its hiring algorithm" to determine whether the AI-enabled recruitment tool produced biased outputs (preferring men over women for certain job categories, for example).[40]

*Who conducts the audit?* Skilled parties within an organization (such as AI developers) or external auditors may conduct the ABA. External parties might include academic researchers, investigative journalists, and/or nonprofit organizations.[41]

---

38. Ada Lovelace Institute, "Examining the Black Box," p. 8, April 29, 2020, https://www.adalovelaceinstitute.org/report/examining-the-black-box-tools-for-assessing-algorithmic-systems/ (last visited March 30, 2025).

39. IAPP, "Key Terms for AI Governance," July 2024, https://iapp.org/resources/article/key-terms-for-ai-governance/ (last visited March 31, 2025). For additional information regarding different types of bias and challenges and guidance on addressing bias in an AI context, see NIST Special Publication 1270, *Towards a Standard for Identifying and Managing Bias in Artificial Intelligence*, March 15, 2022, https://www.nist.gov/publications/towards-standard-identifying-and-managing-bias-artificial-intelligence.

40. Hilke Schellmann, "Auditors Are Testing Hiring Algorithms for Bias, but There's No Easy Fix," *MIT Technology Review*, February 11, 2021, https://www.technologyreview.com/2021/02/11/1017955/auditors-testing-ai-hiring-algorithms-bias-big-questions-remain/ (last visited March 31, 2025). The article notes that the O'Neil Risk Consulting and Algorithmic Auditing (ORCAA) firm also conducts algorithm evaluations. The firm is owned by "Cathy O'Neil, a data scientist and the author of *Weapons of Math Destruction*, one of the seminal popular books on AI bias, who has advocated for AI audits for years." *Id.*

41. Ada Lovelace Institute, "Examining the Black Box," p. 11, April 29, 2020, https://www.adalovelaceinstitute.org/report/examining-the-black-box-tools-for-assessing-algorithmic-systems/ (last visited March 30, 2025).

2. Algorithm Regulatory Audit (ARA)

   *Description:* A comprehensive, broad inspection, likely of an entire AI system, to determine whether it operates following established rules, laws, regulations, and norms. The audit may assess the code underpinning the algorithm, how it operates within an environment (the context), and the organizational process and human behavior (AI governance).[42] For example, an AI system may be evaluated for compliance with data protection, AI, and privacy laws, among others. The *International Journal of Government Auditing* provides an audit framework for government and private-sector organizations to use to assess whether "algorithms meet specified quality criteria, and whether or not the attendant risks have been properly identified and mitigated."[43]

   *Who conducts the audit?* External parties, notably governmental regulators or professional auditors.

3. Algorithmic Risk Assessments (ARKA)

   *Description:* A predeployment assessment of possible impacts and potential harms to society from the AI system and accompanying risks. For example, government regulators may require ARKAs of automatic decision systems "to ensure public accountability."[44] The Integrity Institute provides a framework for risk assessments of algorithmic components of platforms, for example, and accompanying material explaining how "risk assessments can be leveraged as an effective tool for

42. *Id.* at p. 13. A regulator or professional auditor could mandate "access to data about the algorithm's users, inspecting how the system is operating, speaking with developers or users, or looking at code underpinning an algorithmic system." *Id.*

43. Dr. Esther Meijer-van Leijsen, "Developing an Audit Framework for Algorithms," *International Journal of Government Auditing*, Q2 2021, https://www.intosaijournal.org/journal-entry/developing-an-audit-framework-for-algorithms/ (last visited March 31, 2025).

44. Ada Lovelace Institute, "Examining the Black Box," p. 16, April 29, 2020, https://www.adalovelaceinstitute.org/report/examining-the-black-box-tools-for-assessing-algorithmic-systems/ (last visited March 30, 2025).

accountability, transparency and ultimately harm reduction."[45]

*Who conducts the audit?* AI developers, purchasers/users of AI systems, policymakers, and government regulators.

4. Algorithmic Impact Evaluations (AIE)

   *Description:* A postdeployment impact assessment of possible harm to a target population (e.g., adverse impacts on human rights).[46] According to the Institute of Electrical and Electronics Engineers (IEEE), an AIE is an "evaluation of the AI system and its effects on its subjects after it has been launched into the world."[47]

   *Who conducts the audit?* Academic researchers, policymakers, and government regulators.

These audit methods may identify, mitigate, avoid, and/or transfer AI-related risks, but organizations require a holistic approach to institutionalizing AI governance. To accomplish this, an organization needs to select and implement an AI governance framework. Industry best practice is to adopt an AI governance framework—such as the NIST Artificial Intelligence Risk Management Framework (AI RMF) or the ISO/IEC FDIS23894

45. Integrity Institute, "On Risk Assessment and Mitigation for Algorithmic Systems," February 29, 2024, https://integrityinstitute.org/news/institute-news/risk-assessment (last visited March 31, 2025).

46. Ada Lovelace Institute, "Examining the Black Box," p. 18, April 29, 2020, https://www.adalovelaceinstitute.org/report/examining-the-black-box-tools-for-assessing-algorithmic-systems/ (last visited March 30, 2025).

47. Gabriela Bar, Gabriela Wiktorzak & Jeanna Matthews, "Four Conditions for Building Trusted AI Systems," IEEE, July 13, 2021, https://standards.ieee.org/beyond-standards/four-conditions-for-building-trusted-ai-systems/ (last visited March 31, 2025). The article notes that the four conditions for building trusted AI systems are effectiveness, competence, accountability, and transparency.

Information Technology Artificial Intelligence, Guidance on risk management—to manage AI-related risks.[48]

Figure 3 illustrates an example of core components included in an AI governance and risk management program. The program includes foundational strategic documents (AI strategy and policies) as well as tactical documents (implementation plans). Also included are a variety of specific algorithmic risk identification (AI inventory/registry) and risk mitigation (algorithmic impact assessment, algorithmic audit) measures to bring transparency to the opaque "black box."

Policy templates are included in the appendices. Appendix A includes an AI Governance and Risk Management Policy template. Appendix B includes an AI Acceptable Use Policy template. Appendix C includes Ten Steps to Develop an AI Policy. Appendix D includes an AI Policy Template.

48. National Institute of Standards and Technology (NIST), "AI Risk Management Framework FAQs," March 18, 2025, https://www.nist.gov/itl/ai-risk-management-framework/ai-risk-management-framework-faqs. *See also* International Organization for Standardization and the International Electrotechnical Commission (ISO/IEC) FDIS 23894, Information Technology—Artificial Intelligence—Guidance on Risk Management, January 26, 2023, https://www.iso.org/standard/77304.html (last visited March 2, 2025).

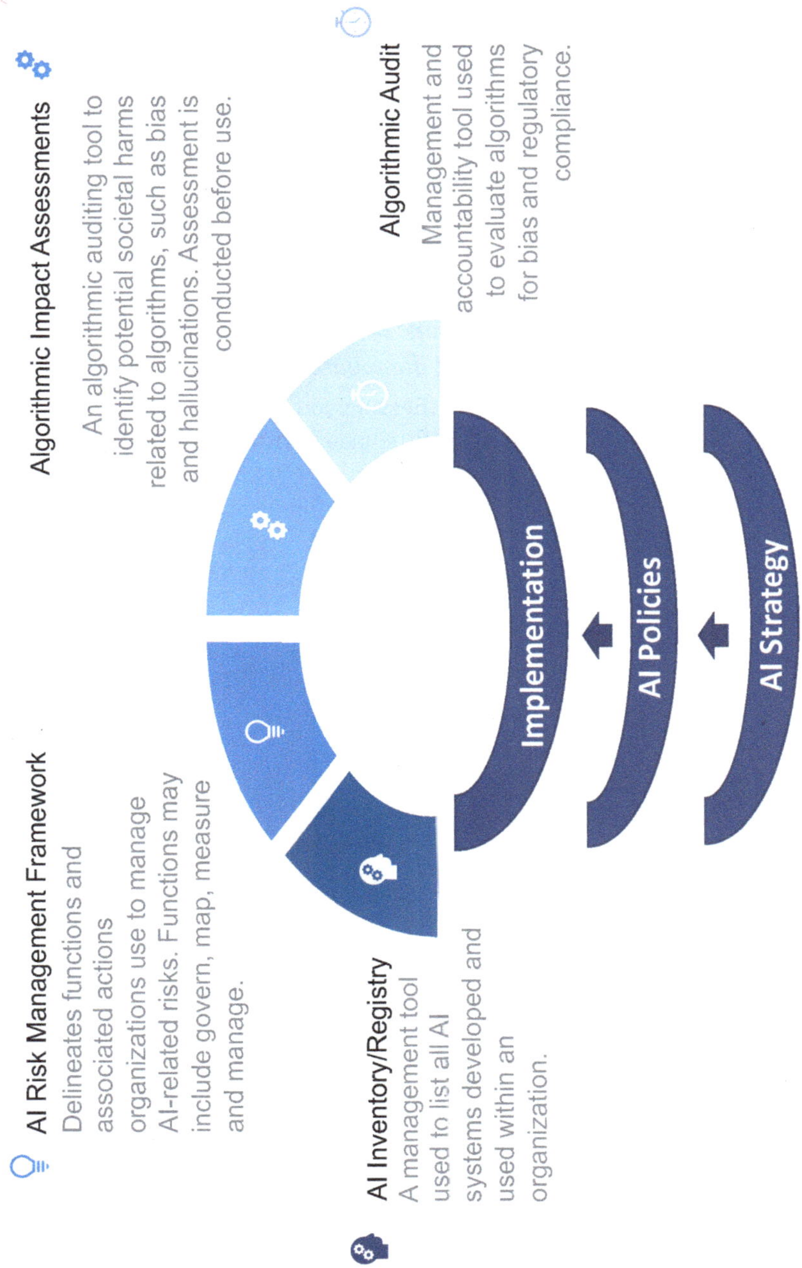


Figure 3: Example of Core Components of an AI Governance and Risk Management Program

*"Companies have tons and tons of data, but [success] isn't about data collection; it's about data management and insight."*

—Prashanth Southekal, professor and head of the Data for Business Performance Institute[49]

49. Beth Stackpole, "10 Best Practices for Analytics Success (Including 3 You Can't Ignore)," MIT Sloan School of Management, September 22, 2020, https://mitsloan.mit.edu/ideas-made-to-matter/10-best-practices-analytics-success-including-3-you-cant-ignore (last visited March 30, 2025).

# V

# The Importance of Data Management

Data are the lifeblood of algorithms, and algorithms are the lifeblood of AI. Ensuring that quality, timely, and trustworthy data are sourced for algorithm development is essential to the complex data integration required for AI systems and to ensure trust in AI outputs. As one Google research team member noted, "Everyone wants to do the model work, not the data work," but given AI-associated risks, prioritizing data management is key to accurate, meaningful AI model outputs.[50]

Despite data management's critical, foundational role in supporting AI, most organizations do not have a comprehensive data management strategy and implementation plan detailing how data are collected, organized, shared, used, stored, and decommissioned. Data management is the industry term for organizing data, which involves "planning, specifying, enabling, creating, acquiring, maintaining, using, archiving,

50. Roger Hoerl & Thomas Redman, "What Managers Should Ask About AI Models and Data Sets," *MIT Sloan Management Review*, December 19, 2023, https://sloanreview.mit.edu/article/what-managers-should-ask-about-ai-models-and-data-sets/ (last visited March 30, 2025).

retrieving, controlling, and purging data."[51] For example, a 2023 McKinsey & Company survey of more than 80 global organizations across industries found that most respondents used siloed data systems and disjointed data management practices.[52] These practices often lead to data incompleteness, inconsistency, and inaccuracy, undermining an organization's readiness to integrate AI into operations.

These practices can also lead to downstream AI-related risk for the organization. "Many organizations still struggle with fundamental data challenges that are exacerbated by the demand for generative AI, which requires ever more data, leading to yet more data management headaches."[53] Generative AI models use "neural networks to identify the patterns and structures within existing data to generate new and original content."[54] These models can be trained to ingest and produce video, text, and images or other types of data. Meta's Llama 3.3, OpenAI's GPT-4o, and Anthropic's Claude 3.5 Sonnet are all examples of generative AI. But, as noted previously, to be prepared to introduce AI, organizations must first "organize [their] information architecture to make their data accessible and usable."[55] See Figure 4 for an example of key industry data management best practices.

---

51. Thor Olavsrud, "What Is Data Governance? Frameworks, Tools, and Best Practices to Manage Data Assets," CIO.com, December 27, 2024, https://www.cio.com/article/202183/what-is-data-governance-a-best-practices-framework-for-managing-data-assets.html (last visited March 25, 2025). Data management may also be referred to as "data resource management or enterprise information management (EIM)." *Id.*

52. McKinsey & Company, "Master Data Management: The Key to Getting More from Your Data," May 15, 2024, https://www.mckinsey.com/capabilities/mckinsey-digital/our-insights/master-data-management-the-key-to-getting-more-from-your-data#/ (last visited March 21, 2025).

53. IBM, "What Is Data Management?," July 3, 2024, https://www.ibm.com/think/topics/data-management (last visited March 19, 2025).

54. NVidia Corporation, "What Is Generative AI?," https://www.nvidia.com/en-us/glossary/generative-ai/ (last visited March 18, 2025).

55. IBM, "What Is Data Management?," July 3, 2024, https://www.ibm.com/think/topics/data-management (last visited March 19, 2025).

Figure 4: Industry Example of Key Data Management Best Practices

Data management encompasses technical (e.g., data standards, information technology data architecture, etc.), operational (e.g., the process of delivering goods/services), and administrative (i.e., the process of managing the organization's internal resources practices). Data governance, data plan and design, data architecture, and data risk management are major components of data management (see Figure 5: Industry-Defined Major Components of Data Management).

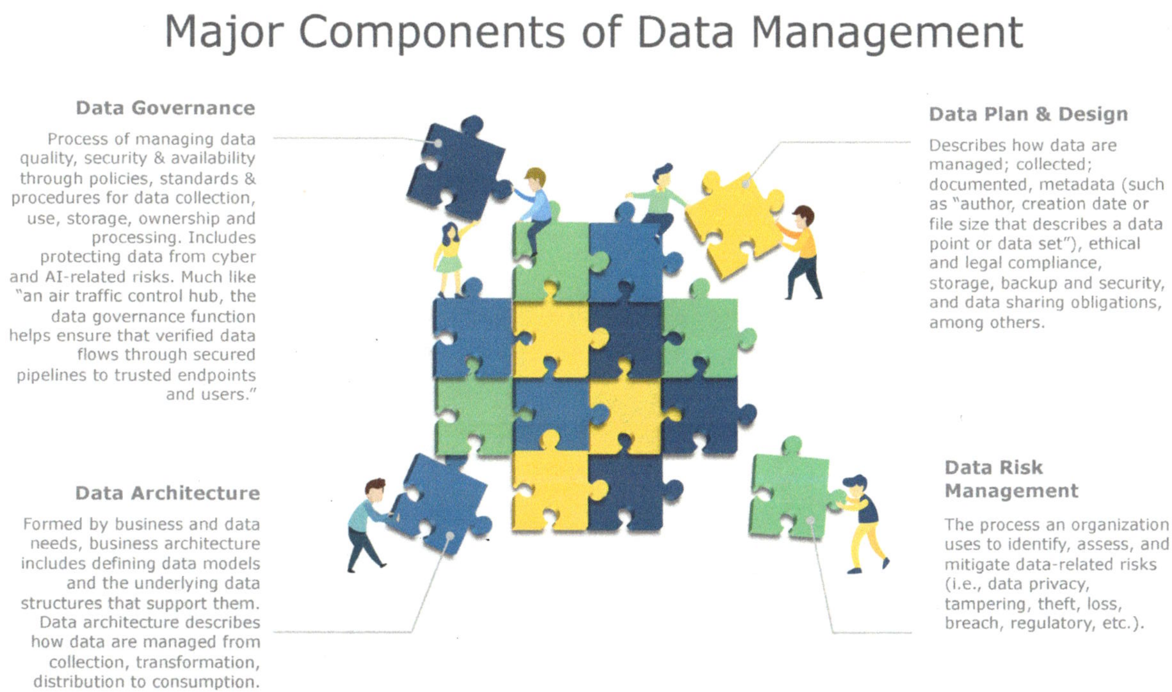


**Figure 5: Industry-Defined Major Components of Data Management**

Source 1: IBM, "What Is a Data Architecture?," https://www.ibm.com/think/topics/data-architecture (last visited March 25, 2025); IBM, "What Is Data Governance?," September 10, 2024, https://www.ibm.com/think/topics/data-governance (last visited March 24, 2025); National Institute of Standards and Technology, "Data Governance and Management (DGM) Profile," December 11, 2024, https://www.nist.gov/privacy-framework/new-projects/data-governance-and-management-profile (last visited March 24, 2025); Data Administration Management Association (DAMA), "DMBOK®2R Wheel Images," 2024, https://www.dama.org/cpages/dmbok2r-wheels (last visited March 25, 2025).

Data management is mainly about having the right data available to the right people at the right time. Are the data fit for purpose—"for a given decision, operation, or analysis"?[56] The MIT Sloan School of Management suggests six criteria for determining whether the data are the "right data" to solve the problem.[57]

1. Does the data have predictive power?
   - Include all attributes that could support predictive characteristics. For example, if the algorithm is designed to predict an individual's credit score, then data related to timeliness of bill payments, total debt-to-income ratio, and late payment occurrences over a specific period of time would all support the predictive power of the credit score algorithm.
2. Does the data adequately address the target population? And, if so, is the volume of data sufficient to train the AI model?
   - Include a comprehensive sample set of data that is representative of the target population as well as the correct volume of data to secure the "right data."
3. Are the data biased based on gender, age, race, or ethnicity, for example?
   - To avoid biased AI outputs, data set inputs need to be free from bias.
4. What span of time should the data reflect?
   - To avoid errors in AI output, specify data range of time.
5. Are all terms defined, including units of measure, to avoid misinterpretation and confusion?
6. What data are excluded (e.g., personally identifiable information, copyrighted works, etc.)?

Much like algorithmic oversight, data management is an ongoing process, not a static one, and must be continuously updated to reflect the changing needs and demands of the operating environment.

---

56. Roger Hoerl & Thomas Redman, "What Managers Should Ask About AI Models and Data Sets," *MIT Sloan Management Review*, December 19, 2023, https://sloanreview.mit.edu/article/what-managers-should-ask-about-ai-models-and-data-sets/ (last visited March 30, 2025).

57. *Id.*

*"Data is at the core of computational systems; it is necessary to train algorithms—without it, algorithms have no basis with which to recognize patterns, perform predictive analysis, or make decisions."*[58]

58. Lydia Kostopoulos, "The Role of Data in Algorithmic Decision-Making: A Primer," United Nations Institute for Disarmament Research, https://unidir.org/files/publication/pdfs/the-role-of-data-in-algorithmic-decision-making-en-815.pdf (last visited March 31, 2025). Kostopoulos is the former director for Strategic Engagement, College of Information and Cyberspace, National Defense University.

# VI

# The AI Development Life Cycle and Due Diligence

Like almost everything in information technology, software development, and information security, AI follows a development life cycle or series of steps. The AI development life cycle is an iterative process that begins with the problem to be solved (design), followed by preparing the data sets for the model (develop), then deploying the model in the environment and continuously monitoring it for accuracy once operationally deployed. Each stage, from problem definition to continuous monitoring, plays a key role in preparing for, deploying, and overseeing AI systems in an operating environment (see Figure 6: Four Steps to AI Development Life Cycle: Design, Develop, Deploy, and Continuous Monitoring).

Two of the most important questions to ask the AI developer during the design phase are: What problem is the developer trying to solve? Does the answer align with the individual's and/or organization's expectations? If not, this could signal a fundamental misunderstanding and needs to be corrected prior to moving on to the next stage—develop.

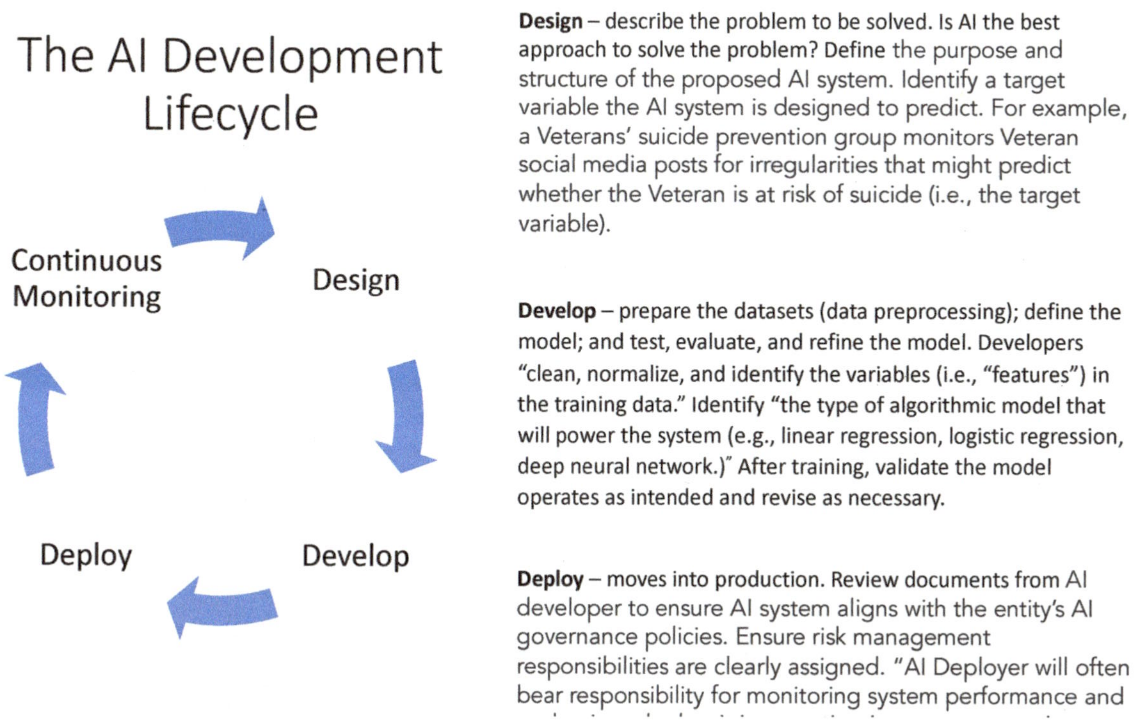


**Figure 6: Four Steps to AI Development Life Cycle: Design, Develop, Deploy, and Continuous Monitoring**

Source 2: Business Software Alliance, "Confronting Bias: BSA's Framework to Build Trust in AI," pp. 16–17, June 8, 2021, https://www.bsa.org/reports/confronting-bias-bsas-framework-to-build-trust-in-ai (last visited March 20, 2025); U.S. Gov't Accountability Off., GAO-21-519SP, Artificial Intelligence: An Accountability Framework for Federal Agencies and Other Entities, pp. 15–16 (2021).

**Note:** Bias may occur throughout the algorithm life cycle:

- **Data inputs:** If training data sets are not comprehensive, timely, or "representative of the populations to which the algorithm will be applied, groups may not be properly represented in the data sets, resulting in disproportionate impacts."[59]
- **In algorithm:** "Flawed assumptions, inappropriate modeling techniques, coding errors, and pattern misidentification in the design process can lead to biased outputs."
- **In use:** "Misinterpreting algorithm outputs, inappropriate use of those outputs (for example, automation bias) and disregarding underlying assumptions can create bias."

Data preprocessing is a large part of the "develop" phase. (See Example Data Preprocessing below.) It is significant because once this step is complete, the data are incorporated into the LLM, which, in turn, impacts the quality of LLM performance. For example, in a clinical setting, preprocessing data sets "must be remarkably accurate" because data inputs provided to AI models "may influence clinical decisions."[60] To address this risk, clinicians and bioinformaticians collaborate to provide the required clinical context to the mathematical algorithm.[61] Identifying risks associated with data preprocessing is key to preventing or mitigating downstream AI model–related output risks (e.g., bias, hallucinations, etc.). Hallucinations refer to "instances in which generative AI models create seemingly plausible but factually incorrect outputs under the appearance of fact."[62]

59. New Zealand Government, "Algorithm Impact Assessment User Guide," https://data.govt.nz/docs/algorithm-impact-assessment-user-guide (last visited June 3, 2025). *See also* U.S. Gov't Accountability Off., GAO-21-519SP, Artificial Intelligence: An Accountability Framework for Federal Agencies and Other Entities, pp. 44–46 (2021).

60. Valentina Bellini et al., "Understanding Basic Principles of Artificial Intelligence: A Practical Guide for Intensivists," *Acta Biomedica: Atenei Parmensis* 93.5 (2022): e2022297, https://pmc.ncbi.nlm.nih.gov/articles/PMC9686179/.

61. *Id.*

62. IAPP, "Key Terms for AI Governance," July 2024, https://iapp.org/resources/article/key-terms-for-ai-governance/ (last visited March 31, 2025).

Example Data Preprocessing[63]

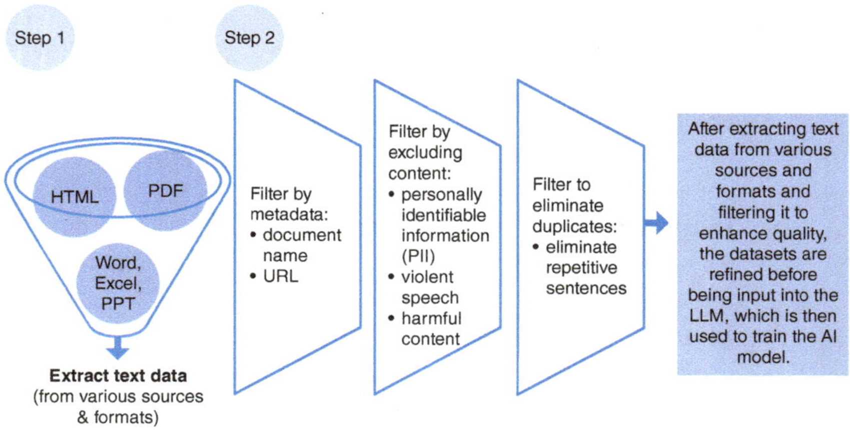


Another key question to identify avoidable risks concerns training data. Training data are data actually used to train the model, regardless of whether it aligns with the "right data" (see Section V, "The Importance of Data Management," for more details regarding the "right data").[64] Specifically, ask the developer, "How will you acquire training data?"[65] The training data may or may not follow the six criteria mentioned previously (see Chapter V, The Importance of Data Management). Compare the training data with the "right data" criteria to identify the delta and assess whether it represents a significant risk to AI model output. Given that there is no such thing as perfect data, expect there to be a delta. Generally, developers provide plans to address/close the delta.[66]

63. Simon Zamarin, David Ping & Vikram Elango et al., "An Introduction to Preparing Your Own Dataset for LLM Training," *AWS Machine Learning Blog*, December 19, 2024, https://aws.amazon.com/blogs/machine-learning/an-introduction-to-preparing-your-own-dataset-for-llm-training/ (last visited March 21, 2025).

64. Roger Hoerl & Thomas Redman, "What Managers Should Ask About AI Models and Data Sets," *MIT Sloan Management Review*, December 19, 2023, https://sloanreview.mit.edu/article/what-managers-should-ask-about-ai-models-and-data-sets/ (last visited March 30, 2025).

65. *Id.*

66. *Id.*

To address the delta, ask the developer these questions:[67]

- "What steps have you taken to understand the full history, subtlety, advantages, and limitations of the training data acquired?"
- "How does it compare to the right data criteria?"

In addition to data preprocessing, data labeling for training some LLMs is key to the quality of AI model performance. Data labeling "plays a crucial role because it directly controls and impacts the quality of responses a model produces."[68] Generally, the most common approach to data labeling involves teams of people labeling data "for various tasks, such as general question-answering, sentiment analysis, summarization, comparing various texts for similarity and differences, and so on."[69] This process is still the most common method used to label data for some LLMs today.[70] Unsurprisingly, the human-based data labeling process may introduce bias into the LLM even as "human labeling is regarded as the gold standard for collecting high-quality data at scale."[71] Thus, the human-based process of labeling data sets may impact the quality of some LLM outputs and present another potential risk to consider when evaluating AI model performance.

---

67. *Id.*
68. *Id.*
69. *Id.*
70. *Id.*
71. *Id.* Note: LLM assisted labeling is another common data labeling approach.

*"Like gods, these mathematical models were opaque, their workings invisible to all but the highest priests in their domain: mathematicians and computer scientists."*[72]

---

72. Dr. Cathy O'Neil, PhD, data scientist and author of *Weapons of Math Destruction*.

# VII

# What's in the "Black Box"? The Importance of Algorithmic Transparency

One of the earliest, most memorable real-world examples of misuse of AI technology came in 2018 when Cambridge Analytica, a UK-based political consulting firm, was accused of psychological manipulation and nonconsensual acquisition and use of personal data of approximately 90 million Facebook (now Meta) users.[73] In 2018, a Cambridge Analytica whistleblower exposed the firm's illicit gathering and use of "people's [Facebook] psychological profiles to influence their political decisions."[74] Cambridge Analytica offered the UK Leave campaign leaders, for example, personalized, psychographic microtargeting campaign ads "to persuade key audience groups to

73. Jason Fernando, "Cambridge Analytica: Overview, History, and Example," Investopedia.com, January 28, 2025, https://www.investopedia.com/terms/c/cambridge-analytica.asp (last visited March 17, 2025).

74. *Id.*

measurably change their behaviour."[75] Investigators found that AI models and the data sets and algorithms underpinning them created a tailored, highly manipulative, steady series of videos, social media posts, and other outreach techniques that likely persuaded enough voters in the UK to leave the EU in a referendum held in June 2016. This is likely the first globally recognized example of how AI and the underlying algorithms—the "black box"—can be used for nefarious purposes. The firm declared bankruptcy in 2018.

As the preceding story illustrates, model developers choose how to design models and what data to use to train AI models. These choices are, in turn, embedded in the code that powers AI models. In the case of Cambridge Analytica, for example, model developers decided to include the psychological and personal data of select Facebook users in the design of AI models. The choices model developers make encode "human prejudices, misunderstandings, and bias into the software systems that increasingly manage our lives."[76] Thus, AI model transparency—describing the underlying algorithmic "logic and reasoning, the data inputs used to train the model, the methods used for model evaluation and validation and more"—is essential to understand the degree and origins of risk (such as bias) and trust in AI systems and outcomes.[77] Transparency also "connotes a kind of quality to information that is about the visibility of information but also its meaningfulness or actionability to involved actors."[78] In other words, transparency without con-

75. Cambridge Analytica, "Leave.EU: Psychographic Targeting for Britain," https://r.search.yahoo.com/_ylt=AwrhboNN4lto8AEAzWFXNyoA;_ylu=Y29sbwNiZjEEcG9zAzYEdnRpZAMEc2VjA3Ny/RV=2/RE=1752061773/RO=10/RU=https%3a%2f%2fia801000.us.archive.org%2f28%2fitems%2fciv53332855%2fBK-Background-paper-CA-proposals-to-LeaveEU.pdf/RK=2/RS=hQHp0h7RjRvgyqVM1jPUP_OAsJQ- (last visited May 14, 2025).

76. Cathy O'Neil, *Weapons of Math Destruction* 3 (2016).

77. Alexandra Jonker, Amanda McGrath & Alice Gomstyn, "What Is AI Transparency?," IBM, September 6, 2024, https://www.ibm.com/think/topics/ai-transparency (last visited March 20, 2025).

78. Daron Acemoglu, "Harms of AI," in Justin B. Bullock et al. (eds.), *The Oxford Handbook of AI Governance*, p. 480, Oxford University Press (2024).

text does not meet the meaning of the term. "Transparency is not just a feature of the technology that speaks for itself without human context . . . . Transparency depends on whether information reveals the intentions of the designers and whether the information is actionable for the receipt of the information, and the user."[79]

## Focus on Algorithmic Development Process to Identify Potential Risk

Algorithms are not objective. Rather, they "reflect the decisions made by the human agents both during its creation and its subsequent use."[80] The subjectivity inherent in algorithmic models calls for methods to understand the "black box" of model decision-making and the potential impact of those outcomes.[81] For example, researchers could use two methods—Shapley Additive exPlanations (SHAP) and Local Interpretable Model-Agnostic Explanations (LIME)—to understand model development. Generally, SHAP is used "to understand the whole model and feature dependencies," while LIME is used "to get a better explanation of a single prediction" from AI model outputs.[82]

In addition to the SHAP and LIME methods used to understand model outcomes, researchers observe five points during algorithm development where humans intentionally or unintentionally may manifest bias or discrimination in the data sets used to train AI models.

---

79. *Id.*

80. B. Custers & E. Fosch-Villaronga (eds.), *Law and Artificial Intelligence: Regulating AI and Applying AI in Legal Practice*, p. 196, T.M.C. Asser Press (2022).

81. Valentina Bellini et al., "Understanding Basic Principles of Artificial Intelligence: A Practical Guide for Intensivists," *Acta Biomedica: Atenei Parmensis* 93.5 (2022): e2022297, https://pmc.ncbi.nlm.nih.gov/articles/PMC9686179/.

82. *Id.*

> *"Being transparent about AI means being honest about what a system is intended to do, where it fits with the organization's overall strategy, which benefits and pitfalls it brings and how it is likely to impact people. It also means explaining why an AI model makes the decisions it does."*[83]

## 1. Defining the Outcome and Class Labels of the AI Model

Identifying the target variables or outcomes, possible classifications, and values shapes the algorithm's operation. Human programmers lead this process and may intentionally or unintentionally introduce bias and/or discrimination into the process. "Target variables may reflect inherent prejudices or faulty assumptions that can perpetuate harmful biases."[84] For example, a retailer uses its application to analyze consumers' purchasing history to monitor for new patterns of behavior that might predict whether a person is expecting a child (i.e., the target variable). While a shopper might deviate from historical purchasing patterns by beginning to buy baby items, that person may not be expecting a child. That person might be purchasing items for a friend, a family member, and/or a charity. The target variable, however, may falsely assume a pregnancy and begin to push baby-related incentives and content to the consumer. Here, the target variable and, by extension, the algorithmic operations are incorrect, leading to incorrect outcomes for the consumer.

## 2. Defining the Training Data and Data Collection for the AI Model

Data sets are the lifeblood of algorithms and, as such, form the foundation of AI model outputs (e.g., predictions, decisions, recommendations, etc.). Thus, AI model outputs will be biased

---

83. World Economic Forum, "Why Transparency Is Key to Unlocking AI's Full Potential," January 2, 2025.

84. Business Software Alliance, "Confronting Bias: BSA's Framework to Build Trust in AI," p. 15, June 8, 2021, https://www.bsa.org/reports/confronting-bias-bsas-framework-to-build-trust-in-ai (last visited March 20, 2025).

or discriminatory if data sets are biased or discriminatory. Humans may, intentionally or unintentionally, introduce bias into training data in at least four ways:[85]

1. selecting "a feature [variable] that benefits one group over another . . .";[86]
2. erroneously classifying and labeling data;
3. statistically, underrepresenting or overrepresenting some groups in the data collected, which, in turn, distorts "the representation of reality by the algorithm";[87] and
4. using subjective rather than objective variables. A variable is a quantity or value that can change. For example, in the formula for risk: risk (r) equals probability (p) times severity (s). Here, the variables are the (p) and (s), which, when multiplied together, result in the (r). It stands to reason that a higher value of either or both of the variables (p) and (s) results in higher (r).

## 3. Selecting the Features to Include in the Algorithm

Feature selection includes determining, for example, "what elements, aspects, abilities, and so forth" should form the algorithm analysis.[88] Features that are "very general" may lack representative qualities, while others may "be chosen to achieve a discriminatory effect."[89] For example, a visa application screening AI model may include "nationality" as a feature. The AI model outcome intentionally discriminates against applicants from "countries of concern." Countries of concern may pose a risk to national security and warrant additional scrutiny.

---

85. B. Custers & E. Fosch-Villaronga (eds.), *Law and Artificial Intelligence: Regulating AI and Applying AI in Legal Practice*, p. 196, T.M.C. Asser Press (2022).
86. *Id.*
87. *Id.*
88. *Id.* at p. 197.
89. *Id.*

## 4. Selecting the Proxies

AI developers "sometimes use proxies as a stand-in for protected attributes, like race or gender, [which] . . . can be unintentionally biased as they might have a false or accidental correlation with the sensitive attributes they were meant to replace."[90] Education attainment, for example, may be used in an algorithm as a proxy for income level, which could, in turn, unfairly disadvantage certain groups whose education attainment is associated with specific racial demographics.[91]

## 5. Developing the Masking

AI developers use "masking" to selectively hide or block inputs, "allowing a neural network to focus on specific areas of interest."[92] In essence, the "mask" acts as a filter, sorting through information to be considered and ignored by the neural network.[93] Developing the masking is important because it allows the AI models to "effectively prioritize and process relevant features, patterns, or objects while discarding unnecessary or less important details," resulting in "more accurate predictions . . . ."[94]

Applied to computer vision, for example, AI masking enables "precise editing and manipulation of specific parts of an image, enhancing tasks such as object recognition and segmentation."[95] Computer vision is "a field of AI that enables computers to process and analyze images, videos, and other visual inputs."[96] Examples of computer vision applications include, but are not

---

90. Alexandra Jonker & Julie Rogers, "What Is Algorithmic Bias?," IBM, September 20, 2024, https://www.ibm.com/think/topics/algorithmic-bias (last visited March 21, 2025).

91. B. Custers & E. Fosch-Villaronga (eds.), *Law and Artificial Intelligence: Regulating AI and Applying AI in Legal Practice*, p. 199, T.M.C. Asser Press (2022).

92. Alooba Pty Ltd., "What Is Mask in Deep Learning?," https://www.alooba.com/skills/concepts/deep-learning/mask/ (last visited March 20, 2025).

93. *Id.*

94. *Id.*

95. Don Cowen, "Masking," *The Science of Machine Learning & AI*, https://www.ml-science.com/masking (last visited March 21, 2025).

96. IAPP, "Key Terms for AI Governance," July 2024, https://iapp.org/resources/article/key-terms-for-ai-governance/ (last visited March 31, 2025).

limited to, facial recognition technology, augmented reality, medical imaging, and autonomous vehicles.

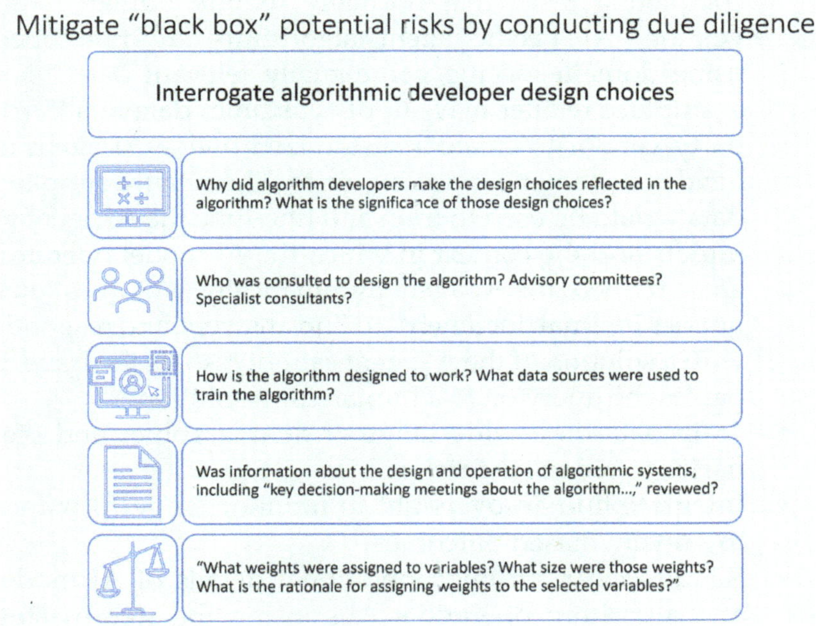


Source: Daron Acemoglu, "Harms of AI," in Justin B. Bullock et al. (eds.), *The Oxford Handbook of AI Governance*, pp. 467–68, Oxford University Press (2024).

## Algorithmic Development: Checklist of Risk Mitigation Measures

- Ensure the goals of the algorithm are stated clearly and expressed with mathematical precision[97]
- Identify the variables used in training the AI model
- Evaluate the methods and performance of AI models continuously to identify and "remove biases emerging from historical data or structure inequity . . ."[98]

---

97. Daron Acemoglu, "Harms of AI," in Justin B. Bullock et al. (eds.), *The Oxford Handbook of AI Governance*, p. 465, Oxford University Press (2024).

98. B. Custers & E. Fosch-Villaronga (eds.), *Law and Artificial Intelligence: Regulating AI and Applying AI in Legal Practice*, p. 188, T.M.C. Asser Press (2022).

- Use domain-specific AI agents to reduce the likelihood of bias. An AI agent is a system or program that works autonomously on behalf of a user or another system, completing tasks that normally require human intervention. AI-specific agent algorithms are fine-tuned using domain-specific, contextually relevant data.[99] For example, a retailer may supply customer data to a third-party vendor to create a customized online AI agent to handle customer service inquiries. The retailer-supplied data would be used to train and fine-tune the AI agent to understand the context in which the AI model operates. Once trained, the AI agent automatically asks questions, queries internal documents to find answers, and responds with a solution. If the AI agent cannot resolve the issue, it passes the query on to a human for resolution.[100]
- Train data on a wide range of demographics and scenarios to reduce the risk of bias
- Integrate human oversight to monitor AI performance to prevent biased outcomes
- Require clear, written operational details of AI model and algorithm operations, disclosing the step-by-step process for decision-making, predictions, recommendations, and so on
- Require written disclosure of the provenance of data used to train models, including original data sources, data dates, information related to copyright (e.g., licensure agreements), information related to privacy/data protections, and so on

99. Forbes Technology Council, "Addressing AI Bias: Strategies Companies Must Adopt Now," *Forbes Magazine*, March 10, 2025, https://www.forbes.com/councils/forbestechcouncil/2025/03/10/addressing-ai-bias-strategies-companies-must-adopt-now/ (last visited May 14, 2025). *See also* Anna Gutowska, "What Are AI Agents?," IBM, July 3, 2024, https://www.ibm.com/think/topics/ai-agents (last visited March 29, 2025) (AI agents "use the advanced natural language processing techniques of large language models (LLMs) to comprehend and respond to user inputs step-by-step and determine when to call on external tools.").

100. Amazon Web Services, "What Are AI Agents?," https://aws.amazon.com/what-is/ai-agents/ (last visited March 29, 2025).

- Perform regular testing and evaluation (red teaming) to identify vulnerabilities, errors, bias, and other potential issues[101]
- Incorporate continuous monitoring to keep abreast of how AI models and systems perform, providing ongoing data to promptly identify and address any issues[102]
- Ensure data are clean, accurate, timely, and uncorrupted before inputting data into the AI model for training. Ensuring data integrity reduces the risk of unreliable outputs, enables a greater likelihood of data traceability, and builds trust in AI model outputs.[103]

## From Opaque to Translucent "Black Box": Questions to Improve Algorithm Quality and Transparency

According to the European Data Protection Supervisor, the vast majority of data sets used to create "state-of-the-art LLMs" were developed using "web scraping, web harvesting, or web data extraction tools"[104] to remove data from public websites, including social media sites, newspapers, journals, and so on.[105] Thus, any information posted on a public website could be amassed to develop training data used to power these LLMs, which are, in turn, powering some of the most popular AI applica-

---

101. Kim Martineua, "What Is Red Teaming for Generative AI?," IBM, April 11, 2024, https://research.ibm.com/blog/what-is-red-teaming-gen-AI (last visited March 29, 2025).

102. *Id.*

103. Forbes Technology Council, "Addressing AI Bias: Strategies Companies Must Adopt Now," *Forbes Magazine*, March 10, 2025, https://www.forbes.com/councils/forbestechcouncil/2025/03/10/addressing-ai-bias-strategies-companies-must-adopt-now/ (last visited May 14, 2025).

104. Tsaone Swaabow Thapelo et al., "SASSCAL WebSAPI: A Web Scraping Application Programming Interface to Support Access to SASSCAL's Weather Data," 20 *Data Sci. J.* 24 (2021). doi: 10.5334/dsj-2021-024.

105. Xabier Lareo, "Large Language Models (LLM)," European Data Protection Supervisor, https://www.edps.europa.eu/data-protection/technology-monitoring/techsonar/large-language-models-llm_en (last visited March 21, 2025).

tions today, such as conversational chatbots. "LLMs are significantly affected by the quality and composition" of the training data, "which is inherently diverse, spanning various domains, sources, and topics."[106]

How accurate are these data sets? How much public data scraped and incorporated into the LLMs contain misinformation? What, if any, controls were in place to filter data sets for accuracy, misinformation, bias, and so on?[107] What controls are in place to filter out sensitive, proprietary, copyrighted, and/or personal information from the data sets used to train the LLM?[108]

Questions in this section are derived from researching select AI-focused academic journals and articles from recognized U.S. universities such as MIT, Stanford, and Harvard, among others, as well as books and newspaper articles. The questions are organized to align with the NIST AI RMF Core's four functions—govern, map, measure, and manage—and select subfunctions to aid the due diligence process. Note that not all of the NIST subfunctions are included in the chart that follows.

The AI RMF Core "provides outcomes and actions that enable dialogue, understanding, and activities to manage AI risks and responsibly develop trustworthy AI systems."[109]

---

106. Jiahui Peng et al., "Unsupervised Topic Models Are Data Mixers for Pre-Training Language Models," arXiv preprint arXiv:2502.16802, February 24, 2025, https://arxiv.org/abs/2502.16802.

107. According to the Business Software Alliance (BSA), the term "bias" may refer to historical, sampling, and/or labeling bias. If the training data sets use past or historic data, those data may reflect historical biases, which may, in turn, create "a risk of further entrenching those inequities." Sampling bias, on the other hand, may emerge if data used to train the AI model is "not representative of the population in which it will be deployed" and thus the outputs may not make accurate predictions "about a member of a class that is either over- or under-represented." And labeling bias refers to mislabeling training data sets, which undermines the AI model's ability "to identify patterns it should be looking for." Business Software Alliance, "Confronting Bias: BSA's Framework to Build Trust in AI," p. 15, June 8, 2021, https://www.bsa.org/reports/confronting-bias-bsas-framework-to-build-trust-in-ai (last visited March 20, 2025).

108. Xabier Lareo, "Large Language Models (LLM)," European Data Protection Supervisor, https://www.edps.europa.eu/data-protection/technology-monitoring/techsonar/large-language-models-llm_en (last visited March 21, 2025).

109. U.S. Department of Commerce, The National Institute of Standards and Technology, "Artificial Intelligence Risk Management Framework 1.0," January 2023, https://doi.org/10.6028/NIST.AI.100-1 (last visited March 13, 2025).

Trustworthy AI, responsible AI, and ethical AI are generally used interchangeably to refer to "principle-based AI development and AI governance, including the principles of security, safety, transparency, explainability, accountability, privacy and nondiscrimination/nonbias . . . , among others."[110] The NIST AI RMF aligns with many elements of the Organisation for Economic Co-operation and Development (OECD) approach to AI, such as the AI life cycle and the definition of key AI terms.

| NIST AI RMF Core Functions | Select NIST AI RMF Core Subfunctions | Questions[111] |
|---|---|---|
| Govern | Legal and regulatory requirements involving AI are understood, managed, and documented. | Does the automated AI system include a "human in the loop," meaning does a human make the decision or the AI system itself? For example, if a physician uses an AI tool when diagnosing a patient, is the physician the final decision-maker, or does the AI tool determine the diagnosis? What is the determinative factor or set of factors that lead to the outcome? If there is a "human in the loop," then is it possible to seek redress for potential harm(s)? If not, it is possible the automated AI system could "deprive individuals of a right to an accountable decision-maker?"[112] |

110. IAPP, "Key Terms for AI Governance," July 2024, https://iapp.org/resources/article/key-terms-for-ai-governance/ (last visited March 31, 2025).

111. Sources referenced to formulate these questions include the NIST AI RMF 1.0; The Stanford Institute for Human-Centered AI (HAI); *MIT Technology Review: The Algorithm*; and Cathy O'Neil, *Weapons of Math Destruction* (2016). HAI-specific references include "Managing Risks in AI-Powered Biomedical Research," February 24, 2025, https://hai.stanford.edu/news/managing-risks-ai-powered-biomedical-research?mc_cid=afbd258c20&mc_eid=110af7c581 (last visited March 16, 2025).

112. Daron Acemoglu, "Harms of AI," in Justin B. Bullock et al. (eds.), *The Oxford Handbook of AI Governance*, p. 465, Oxford University Press (2024).

| NIST AI RMF Core Functions | Select NIST AI RMF Core Subfunctions | Questions[111] |
|---|---|---|
| | The characteristics of trustworthy AI are integrated into organizational policies, processes, procedures, and practices. | Are trustworthy AI characteristics such as valid and reliable, safe, secure, resilient, accountable and transparent, explainable and interpretable, privacy-enhanced, and fair integrated in/reflected in the organization's policies, processes, procedures, and practices? |
| | Mechanisms are in place to inventory AI systems and are resourced according to organizational risk priorities. | Are there adequate resources to "build, test, maintain, and oversee an automated system?"[113] |
| | | Is there enough data storage on and off premises to accommodate AI?[114] Is the computer processing speed adequate?[115] |
| | Organizational practices are in place to enable AI testing, identification of incidents, and information sharing. | Are risk mitigation practices, such as simulating adversarial testing or red teaming, in place to identify potential risks? Are they conducted continuously as warranted by changes to AI systems and/or technologies? |
| Map | All risks and benefits of components of the AI system, including third-party software and data, are mapped.<br><br>See pages 53–56 for more details regarding the "map" function. | What is the approach to mapping AI technologies and associated legal risks, including use of third-party vendors? How is this approach implemented within the organization, including training? Are potential third-party intellectual property infringements accounted for in the documentation? What internal risk controls are in place for components of AI systems, including third-party AI technologies, and are they identified and documented? |

113. *Id.* at p. 470.
114. *Id.*
115. *Id.*

| **NIST AI RMF Core Functions** | **Select NIST AI RMF Core Subfunctions** | **Questions[111]** |
|---|---|---|
| Measure | AI system performance or assurance criteria are measured qualitatively and quantitatively and demonstrated for conditions similar to deployment setting(s). Measures are documented. | Are the data sources audited to identify any potential bias in the AI models? What mitigation steps are taken to address bias if/ when discovered? |
| | | Are the data used to train the algorithm aligned with the population that will be "subject to the outcomes of an automated system"?[116] |
| | | Does documentation describe how training and testing data have been acquired/ collected, prepared, and updated to demonstrate data quality and reliability?[117] |
| | AI system security and resilience are evaluated and documented. | Are cybersecurity assets (monetary and talent) evaluated, documented, and adequate to protect the expanded landscape of potential risk with automated systems? What about data storage protection? What about computer processor protection?[118] |
| | AI system security and resilience are evaluated and documented. | Are assessments of interconnectedness and dependencies of data streams underpinning AI system operations complete?[119] |

116. *Id.* at p. 471. Data quality may be compromised if data changes more quickly than the algorithm can be updated and retrained; then "the algorithm becomes 'brittle' . . . and lacks external validity." For example, an algorithm used for financial forecasting of the U.S. stock market might work well under normal employment and inflation conditions; however, the algorithm may not provide accurate forecasts during an unprecedented period of upheaval, such as a worldwide pandemic. *Id.*

117. U.S. Gov't Accountability Off., GAO-21-519SP, Artificial Intelligence: An Accountability Framework for Federal Agencies and Other Entities, p. 6 (2021).

118. Daron Acemoglu, "Harms of AI," in Justin B. Bullock et al. (eds.), *The Oxford Handbook of AI Governance*, p. 470, Oxford University Press (2024).

119. U.S. Gov't Accountability Off., GAO-21-519SP, Artificial Intelligence: An Accountability Framework for Federal Agencies and Other Entities, p. 6 (2021).

| NIST AI RMF Core Functions | Select NIST AI RMF Core Subfunctions | Questions[111] |
|---|---|---|
| | Risks associated with transparency and accountability are examined and documented. | Do the AI model developer(s) and/or vendor describe how the model works in plain text, including the rationale for weight selection and the origin of the data used to operate the model? |
| Manage | Mechanisms are in place and applied to sustain the value of deployed AI systems. | Are there mechanisms to restrict access to AI models to prevent possible misuse? |
| | Post-deployment AI system monitoring plans are implemented, including mechanisms for capturing and evaluating user input and other relevant AI actors, appeal and override, decommissioning, incident response, recovery, and change management. | Are rules or procedures in place to stop activities and/or suspected bad actors seeking to misuse AI systems? What access control systems are in place? How is access granted, suspended, and/or denied to AI systems? Is there an AI incident response plan? Is incident response training provided such that rules and procedures to stop activities and/or suspected bad actors are well understood among stakeholders (e.g., employees, contractors, others)? |
| | | Are plans in place to continuously and routinely monitor AI systems to ensure they perform as intended?[120] Does the plan describe processes and procedures to continuously monitor the AI systems?[121] Does the plan specify the frequency of monitoring?[122] |

In addition to the preceding questions, of the four NIST AI RMF Core functions, the "Map" function is particularly significant to the due diligence process. This function focuses on context, on "anticipating, assessing, and otherwise addressing

120. *Id.* at p. 61.
121. *Id.* at p. 64.
122. *Id.*

potential sources of negative risk" before introducing AI technologies into an environment.[123] The "Map" function comprises five categories. To help practitioners elicit AI risk–related information, a series of example questions is aligned to each category.

1. **Establish and understand the context in which AI technologies will operate.** For example, what is the intended purpose of using AI? What are the potential benefits and costs? What local, state, and federal laws, regulations, and policies may be triggered? Who will use the AI technologies and systems? What are the potential positive and negative impacts of AI usage on individuals, communities, organizations, society, and the planet? What are the goals of the organization/department/individual in using AI? What is the return on investment—the business case—for using AI? What is the organization's risk tolerance associated with AI technologies? What are the system requirements (e.g., "the system shall respect fundamental human rights such as the right of privacy of its users" and "the system shall respect the health and safety of its users")?[124] Are the system requirements documented and understood by all AI stakeholders?
2. **Categorize the AI systems.** An AI system is machine-based, generating outputs (predictions, recommendations, decisions) for a given set of objectives. "AI systems are designed to operate with varying levels

---

123. The National Institute of Standards and Technology (NIST), "AI Risk Management Framework (AI RMF)," p. 25, January 26, 2023, https://nvlpubs.nist.gov/nistpubs/ai/NIST.AI.100-1.pdf.

124. Regulation (EU) 2024/1689 of the European Parliament and of the Council of 13 June 2024 laying down harmonised rules on artificial intelligence and amending Regulations (EC) No 300/2008, (EU) No 167/2013, (EU) No 168/2013, (EU) 2018/858, (EU) 2018/1139 and (EU) 2019/2144 and Directives 2014/90/EU, (EU) 2016/797 and (EU) 2020/1828 (Artificial Intelligence Act), preamble, 2024, O.J. (L 12.7.), https://eur-lex.europa.eu/legal-content/EN/TXT/?uri=CELEX%3A32024R1689. The preamble of the EU AI Act specifies important context for regulating AI: "As a pre-requisite, artificial intelligence should be a human-centric technology. It should serve as a tool for people, with the ultimate aim of increasing human well-being."

of autonomy."[125] For example, are tasks, activities, and methods to implement AI systems defined or explained (e.g., classifiers, generative models, recommenders)? AI models use classification algorithms to process data sets inputted into the model "against a specified classifier that sets the criteria for how the data should be sorted."[126] For example, an image classifier might categorize pictures of pets using class labels such as dog, cat, bunny, and so on.[127] Are AI system knowledge limits documented? What documents explain how AI system outputs are used and overseen by humans? Is the information provided detailed enough to make informed decisions and take risk-informed actions?

3. **Use appropriate benchmarks to compare AI capabilities, targeted usage, goals, and expected costs and benefits.** For example, is the rationale for selecting the benchmarks clear and understandable to stakeholders/

---

125. The NIST AI RMF refers to an AI system as "an engineered or machine-based system that can, for a given set of objectives, generate outputs such as predictions, recommendations, or decisions influencing real or virtual environments. AI systems are designed to operate with varying levels of autonomy (Adapted from: OECD Recommendation on AI:2019; ISO/IEC 22989:2022)." *See* The National Institute of Standards and Technology (NIST), "AI Risk Management Framework (AI RMF)," p. 1, January 26, 2023, https://nvlpubs.nist.gov/nistpubs/ai/NIST.AI.100-1.pdf. Article 3 of the EU AI Act defines "AI system" as "a machine-based system that is designed to operate with varying levels of autonomy and that may exhibit adaptiveness after deployment, and that, for explicit or implicit objectives, infers, from the input it receives, how to generate outputs such as predictions, content, recommendations, or decisions that can influence physical or virtual environments." *See* Artificial Intelligence Act, *supra* note 124, at Article 3 Definitions. *See also* Annex to the Communication to the Commission Approval of the content of the draft Communication from the Commission—Commission Guidelines on the definition of an artificial intelligence system established by Regulation (EU) 2024/1689 (AI Act) of February 6, 2025, C(2025) 924 final, https://digital-strategy.ec.europa.eu/en/library/commission-publishes-guidelines-ai-system-definition-facilitate-first-ai-acts-rules-application (last visited March 20, 2025).

126. Ivan Belcic, "What Is Classification in Machine Learning?," IBM, https://www.ibm.com/think/topics/classification-machine-learning (last visited March 20, 2025).

127. *Id.*

parties? Have potential monetary and nonmonetary costs been calculated if and when an AI error occurs or if the AI system malfunctions or fails? Have organizational risk tolerance documents been updated to include introducing and using AI technologies and AI systems? Are the risk tolerances set and approved by the appropriate leadership of the organization? Are processes for operator and practitioner proficiency with AI system performance and trustworthiness to relevant AI system technical standards and certifications defined, assessed, and documented? Are the processes detailing human oversight well documented, defined, assessed, and aligned with organizational policies as specified in the "Govern" function of the NIST AI RMF?

4. **Map risks and benefits for all components of the AI system, including third-party software and data.** For example, what is the approach to mapping AI technologies and associated legal risks, including use of third-party vendors? How is this approach implemented within the organization, including training? Are potential third-party intellectual property infringements accounted for in the documentation? What internal risk controls are in place for components of AI systems, including third-party AI technologies, and are they identified and documented?
5. **Characterize the potential impacts of AI systems on individuals, groups, communities, organizations, and society.** What is the likelihood and severity of each AI system's potential impact (both beneficial and harmful) based on expected use, past uses in similar contexts, public incident reports, feedback from external sources that developed or deployed the AI system, or other data identified and documented? What are the established practices to support ongoing outreach to AI stakeholders/parties? What personnel are required to support these practices? How are the data gathered from these potential impacts integrated into the feedback loop?

### Key AI Governance Practices*

**Organizational Level**

- Define clear goals and objectives of using AI systems
- Define clear roles and responsibilities for AI systems
- Establish principles as a first step to develop AI policy
- Recruit a multidisciplinary team of talent
- Integrate a diverse set of stakeholders to identify and mitigate risks
- Develop an AI-specific risk management plan
- Develop an AI-specific incident response plan

**Systems Level**

- Develop written technical specifications to document the intended purpose of AI systems
- Ensure AI systems comply with applicable laws, regulations, standards, and guidance
- Provide access to AI algorithms and system designs, operations, and limitations

*Source: U.S. Gov't Accountability Off., GAO-21-519SP, Artificial Intelligence: An Accountability Framework for Federal Agencies and Other Entities, p. 5 (2021).

*"Who will decide? Who will make the choice to delegate, or not to delegate, responsibility and authority?"*[128]

128. Henry A. Kissinger, Craig Mundie & Eric Schmidt, *Genesis*, p. 217.

# VIII

# Conclusion

Who will decide how AI shall be governed? What nation-state's laws, regulations, and policies will the rest of the world follow? Will cooperation or competition characterize AI investment and innovation among nation-states? These and other questions will surely keep policymakers worldwide engaged in debate. While we wait for consensus, we need governance structures, methods, policies, and practices in place to govern AI technologies and associated risks.

As the book illustrates, AI governance and risk management require thoughtful due diligence, careful interrogation of AI vendors and developers, scrupulous review of contracts for AI technologies and services, and relevant expertise in policy, law, information technology, information security, risk, and data management. It takes a multidisciplinary team of talent to inventory, plan, organize, implement, and monitor an organization's AI governance and risk management program.

Wave after wave of advancements in information technology products and services have led to changes in management practices. Prior to the rapid rise of AI, organizations grappled with cybersecurity risk. Successive waves of change will continue, and the most prepared, most resilient, and most capable organizations and leaders will be those with AI governance and risk management infrastructure (people, process, and technology) in place. In short, AI can be managed—it's not magic, it's math.

### Key Data Management Practices*

- Prioritize data management infrastructure (people, process, and technology)
- Automate the data management process and virtualize data
- Conduct an inventory of existing data assets
- Develop a culture of treating data as a critical, strategic asset
- Develop policies and procedures to manage life cycle of data
- Standardize and integrate data
- Invest in data quality
- Engage stakeholders in the governance process
- Comply with legal and regulatory requirements
- Follow industry best practices
- Consider data event stream processing
- Manage metadata

*Source: Thor Olavsrud, "What Is Data Governance? Frameworks, Tools, and Best Practices to Manage Data Assets," CIO.com, December 27, 2024, https://www.cio.com/article/202183/what-is-data-governance-a-best-practices-framework-for-managing-data-assets.html (last visited March 25, 2025).

# APPENDIX A

## AI Governance and Risk Management Policy Template

This template may be modified and used by general counsels, business consultants, information and security professionals, and others to help manage AI-related risks and detail the roles and responsibilities required to implement safe and secure AI technologies. This template is not generated using AI tools/technologies. It is the result of numerous months of research and experience. Sources are carefully documented in footnotes.

I. Effective date
What date does the policy go into effect? Place that date on the document's first page, along with the publication date. Refer to the effective date in the executive summary and the policy overview.

II. Executive summary
Summarize the document's purpose and the policy's effective date and provide a brief overview of the policy.

III. Purpose
What is the purpose of this document?

IV. Scope
Who is within scope and must adhere to this policy?

V. Waivers and exceptions
Identify any entities that will not have to adhere to this policy.

VI. Authority
Who within the entity (role/department) has the authority to approve the policy and initiate policy changes? For example, the chief executive officer (CEO) and board of directors may approve the policy, while the chief security officer, general counsel, chief information officer, and/or chief risk officer may initiate changes to the policy.

VII. Legal references
Reference any applicable international, federal, state, and local laws, regulations, rules, and policies that may apply. For example, some U.S. entities may need to comply with the European Union Artificial Intelligence Act (EU AI Act), which took effect August 1, 2024, such as "providers, deployers, importers, distributors, and product manufacturers of AI systems . . . seeking to put into service and use" AI systems in the EU market.[129] California, Colorado, and Utah have AI-specific state laws that are applicable to the private sector.[130] If the legal references are extensive, place this section in an appendix.

VIII. Overview of policy
Briefly describe the policy, including potential risks associated with AI systems (referencing an AI risk management framework), prohibited uses of AI, and roles and responsibilities within the entity. "AI system" means a "machine-based system designed to operate with varying

---

129. Tim Hickman et al., "Long Awaited EU AI Act Becomes Law After Publication in the EU's Official Journal," White & Case, LLP, July 16, 2024, https://www.whitecase.com/insight-alert/long-awaited-eu-ai-act-becomes-law-after-publication-eus-official-journal (last visited February 27, 2025).

130. *See* International Association of Privacy Professionals, "State AI Governance Law Chart," February 24, 2025, https://iapp.org/resources/article/us-state-ai-governance-legislation-tracker/#state-ai-governance-law-chart. This tracker focuses on cross-sectoral AI governance bills that apply to private-sector organizations.

levels of autonomy" and may make inferences, predictions, recommendations, and/or decisions from inputs it receives.[131]

a. Summarize potential risks associated with AI systems.[132] Potential risks may include, but are not limited to, the following:
    i. Societal threats—users of AI tools may negatively impact people and organizations within society, causing job displacement and/or loss, for example. Conducting an AI Impact Assessment is one way to use AI more responsibly, strategically, and ethically. An AI Impact Assessment provides a process to analyze the impact an AI system may have on people, organizations, and society.[133]
    ii. Cybersecurity threats—"bad actors can exploit AI to launch cyberattacks" by, for example, "manipulating AI tools to clone voices, generate fake identities, and create convincing phishing emails" in furtherance of another crime such as fraud or theft.[134]
    iii. Data privacy threats—users of AI tools may inadvertently or intentionally share personally identifiable information (PII) or sensitive or confidential information by using an AI technology, such as a conversational chatbot.[135] Sensitive data describes

131. Artificial Intelligence Act, *supra* note 124, at Article 3 Definitions.

132. "AI system" is an "engineered or machine-based system that can, for a given set of objectives, generate outputs such as predictions, recommendations, or decisions influencing real or virtual environments. AI systems are designed to operate with varying levels of autonomy." The National Institute of Standards and Technology (NIST) Trustworthy & Responsible AI Resource Center, "Glossary," https://airc.nist.gov/glossary/ (last visited February 28, 2025).

133. Microsoft, "Microsoft Responsible AI Impact Assessment Template," June 2022, https://blogs.microsoft.com/wp-content/uploads/prod/sites/5/2022/06/Microsoft-RAI-Impact-Assessment-Template.pdf (last visited March 30, 2025).

134. Diane Caballarm Rina, "10 AI Dangers and Risks and How to Manage Them," IBM, September 3, 2024, https://www.ibm.com/think/insights/10-ai-dangers-and-risks-and-how-to-manage-them (last visited February 25, 2025).

135. *Id.*

data that could undermine security if lost, misused, accessed, or modified without authorization.[136] Confidential data are protected "so that unauthorized parties cannot view the data."[137] In addition, "machine-learning algorithms . . . present a distinctive privacy concern in their ability to combine seemingly disparate, non-sensitive data to yield predictions about personal information, such as sexual orientation or political ideology."[138] Machine learning (ML), a branch of AI, enables computers and machines to "learn" without explicitly being programmed.[139] Recommendation algorithms underpin Netflix's platform, driven by ML, which learns what a person prefers to watch and recommends similar entertainment options, for example.[140]

Exposing PII and/or sensitive/confidential information via an AI application may result in that data being included in the underlying AI model used to power the AI application. Thus, the data may be included without the necessary consent from the owner of the PII and/or sensitive/confidential information.

iv. Lack of data quality and/or management—research indicates most firms, governments, and other entities lack data quality and/or management, which, when coupled with AI technologies, may provide a veneer of objective, trusted outputs when in fact

136. The National Institute of Standards and Technology (NIST), Computer Security Resource Center, "Sensitive," https://csrc.nist.gov/glossary/term/sensitive (last visited March 2, 2025).

137. The National Institute of Standards and Technology (NIST), Computer Security Resource Center, "Confidentiality," https://csrc.nist.gov/glossary/term/confidentiality (last visited March 2, 2025).

138. Daron Acemoglu, "Harms of AI," in Justin B. Bullock et al. (eds.), *The Oxford Handbook of AI Governance*, p. 467, Oxford University Press (2024).

139. Sara Brown, "Machine Learning, Explained," MIT Sloan School of Management, April 21, 2021, https://mitsloan.mit.edu/ideas-made-to-matter/machine-learning-explained (last visited March 29, 2025).

140. *Id.*

the poor quality of data input leads to poor quality of outputs. "Data that is outdated, unstable (i.e., will not be available when the [AI] model is applied), or is not representative of the target population should be excluded."[141] Data quality "measures how well datasets meet criteria for accuracy, completeness, validity, consistency, uniqueness, timeliness, and fitness for purpose, and it is critical to all data governance initiatives within an organization."[142]

Equally important is the concept of data management, "the practice of collecting, processing and using data securely and efficiently for better business outcomes" (see section V, "The Importance of Data Management").[143] If the underlying data architecture is characterized by a lack of data management, then introducing AI technologies into the environment will exacerbate existing vulnerabilities and likely introduce new weaknesses that could be exploited.

v. Intellectual property (IP) infringement—AI models underpinning AI tools may include copyright-protected works, such as an artist's picture, which may trigger claims of IP violations. OpenAI and Google, for example, argue they need access to copyrighted content to train models to "avoid

---

141. B. Custers & E. Fosch-Villaronga (eds.), *Law and Artificial Intelligence: Regulating AI and Applying AI in Legal Practice*, pp. 227–28, T.M.C. Asser Press (2022). Models are built using data that are currently available. However, if data are likely not to be, or will not be, available in the future, when the model is expected to be deployed, that data should not be included in the development data.

142. IBM, "What Is Data Quality?," https://www.ibm.com/think/topics/data-quality (last visited February 26, 2025).

143. Jim Holdsworth, "What Is Data Management?," IBM, July 3, 2024, https://www.ibm.com/think/topics/data-management (last visited February 26, 2025).

forfeiting" AI leadership to China.[144] Google argues "fair use policies, along with text and data mining exceptions . . . [are] critical to training AI on publicly available data."[145] As copyright policies continue to develop, one way to address the risk of possible copyright infringement is to include a disclaimer on AI-generated outputs (e.g., "This image was created in whole or in part using a third-party vendor artificial intelligence tool.").

vi. AI incidents—users of AI tools may experience incidents, such as bias,[146] hallucinations, and/or unresponsiveness, when driving AI-assisted vehicles.[147] Managing AI incidents is not necessarily clearly defined in law, policy, or regulation yet, but it is important to develop AI incident response procedures to ensure preparedness if/when AI incidents occur. These procedures should identify who develops the procedures; what the procedures entail; when the procedures are triggered; why the procedures are necessary; and how the procedures are implemented and updated.

vii. Lack of transparency—algorithms and AI models include "internal mechanisms and decision-making

144. Emma Roth, "OpenAI and Google Ask the Government to Let Them Train AI on Content They Don't Own," TheVerge.com, March 14, 2025, https://www.theverge.com/news/630079/openai-google-copyright-fair-use-exception (last visited March 20, 2025).

145. *Id.*

146. Bias in the context of AI models refers to "amplification and exacerbation of historical, societal, and systemic biases; performance disparities between sub-groups or languages, possibly due to non-representative training data, that result in discrimination, amplification of biases, or incorrect presumptions about performance; undesired homogeneity that skews system or model outputs, which may be erroneous, lead to ill-founded decision-making or amplify harmful biases." The National Institute of Standards and Technology (NIST), "AI Risk Management Framework (AI RMF)," p. 4, January 26, 2023, https://nvlpubs.nist.gov/nistpubs/ai/NIST.AI.100-1.pdf.

147. Diane Caballarm Rina, "10 AI Dangers and Risks and How to Manage Them," September 3, 2024, https://www.ibm.com/think/insights/10-ai-dangers-and-risks-and-how-to-manage-them (last visited February 25, 2025).

processes [that] are a mystery, even to AI researchers who work closely with the technology."[148] In addition, "the data on which the algorithm was trained, including its source, scope, quality, and inner correlations," are generally opaque.[149] The opaqueness and complexity of algorithms and AI models may undermine trust in AI-generated outcomes and/or AI-assisted outcomes.[150]

b. AI risk management framework
   i. Has the entity adopted a formal risk management framework to systematically identify, mitigate, and address potential risks associated with AI technologies?[151] Examples of AI risk management frameworks include (in alphabetical order; not an exhaustive list):
      1. European Union (EU) Artificial Intelligence (AI) Act (Regulation (EU) 2024/1689, harmonized rules on artificial intelligence).[152] This is "the first-ever comprehensive legal framework on AI worldwide" that went into force on August 1, 2024, and will be near fully implemented on August 2, 2026.[153] The EU AI Office and "authorities of the Member States are responsible for implementing, supervising and enforcing the [risk-based] AI Act."[154] This

---

148. *Id.*

149. Christopher S. Yoo, "Beyond Algorithmic Disclosure for AI," 25 *Colum. Sci. & Tech. L. Rev.* 314, 314 (2024).

150. For best practices and guidance to secure AI systems, see Microsoft AI Security Risk Assessment, December 9, 2021, https://github.com/Azure/AI-Security-Risk-Assessment/blob/main/AI_Risk_Assessment_v4.1.4.pdf.

151. Annie Badman, "What Is AI Risk Management?," IBM, June 20, 2024, https://www.ibm.com/think/insights/ai-risk-management (last visited February 28, 2025).

152. June 13, 2024, https://digital-strategy.ec.europa.eu/en/policies/regulatory-framework-ai.

153. European Union (EU) Artificial Intelligence (AI) Act (Regulation (EU) 2024/1689 laying down harmonized rules on artificial intelligence), June 13, 2024, https://digital-strategy.ec.europa.eu/en/policies/regulatory-framework-ai.

154. *Id.*

risk-based AI risk management approach is tailored for private-sector implementation.

2. Google Secure AI Framework (SAIF).[155] This framework focuses on security, Artificial Intelligence/Machine Learning model risk management, privacy and compliance, talent, and governance. The framework focuses on reviewing and inventorying current security controls, evaluating those controls against emerging AI threats, analyzing what new security controls need to be added to address AI threats, and preparing to store and track supply chain assets, code, and training data, among others.
3. ISO/IEC 23894:2023, "Information Technology—Artificial Intelligence—Guidance on Risk Management."[156] This voluntary framework helps organizations integrate risk management practices into AI-related activities and functions. In addition, ISO 31000:2018, Clause 5 provides information specific to the development, provisioning, offering, or use of AI systems.
4. The National Institute of Standards and Technology (NIST), "AI Risk Management Framework (AI RMF)."[157] The voluntary, risk-based framework was developed with input from the private and public sectors and is useful for designers, developers, users, and evaluators of AI technologies.[158]

---

155. June 8, 2023, https://safety.google/cybersecurity-advancements/saif/.

156. February 6, 2023, https://www.iso.org/standard/77304.html#lifecycle.

157. January 26, 2023, https://nvlpubs.nist.gov/nistpubs/ai/NIST.AI.100-1.pdf.

158. The National Institute of Standards and Technology (NIST), "AI Risk Management Framework FAQs," February 6, 2025, https://www.nist.gov/itl/ai-risk-management-framework/ai-risk-management-framework-faqs (last visited March 1, 2025).

5. U.S. Department of State, "Risk Management Profile for Artificial Intelligence and Human Rights."[159] This voluntary, risk-based framework was developed for governments, the private sector, and civil society to design, develop, deploy, use, and govern AI consistent with international human rights. The State Department's approach focuses on international human rights because it is foundational to stakeholders across sectors and around the world.[160]

c. AI use restrictions: briefly describe the unacceptable uses of AI tools/technologies in the entity's environment, including AI-enabled or AI-enhanced processes, procedures, and/or outcomes. A high-level summary of OpenAI's use policy in Figure 7, for example, showcases types of behaviors prohibited by OpenAI when using any of its services (ChatGPT, abs.openai.com, and the OpenAI API).

In contrast, DeepSeek's use policy is much broader in scope and contains a higher level of detail than OpenAI's policy. A high-level summary of DeepSeek's use policy in Figure 8 showcases, for example, a wider range of prohibited behaviors when using DeepSeek and its array of services.

Typically, an acceptable use policy details restricted uses by such language as:

> "Refrain from using AI in any manner that violates domestic or international laws . . . . Do not use AI in a manner or for purposes that pose unacceptable levels of risk. Consistent with these goals, . . . **[employees/**

---

159. July 25, 2024, https://2021-2025.state.gov/risk-management-profile-for-ai-and-human-rights/.

160. U.S. Department of State, "Risk Management Profile for Artificial Intelligence and Human Rights," July 25, 2024, https://2021-2025.state.gov/risk-management-profile-for-ai-and-human-rights/ (last visited March 1, 2025).

| Company | Service Usage Policies (Rules that apply to users of the services) | | | |
|---|---|---|---|---|
| | Comply with applicable laws (i.e. privacy, prohibited illegal activities) | Prohibited from using services to harm yourself or others | Prohibited from using output from services to harm others (i.e., using output to scam, defraud, bully) | Prohibited from circumventing safeguards or safety mitigations |
| OpenAI | ✓ | ✓ | ✓ | ✓ |

| Company | Service Usage Policies (Rules that apply to users of the services) | | | |
|---|---|---|---|---|
| | Comply with applicable laws (more expansive & includes regulations, regulatory policies, legitimate rights and interests of third parties) | Prohibited from using services to harm yourself or others | Prohibited from using output from services to harm others (i.e., using output to scam, defraud, bully) | Prohibited from circumventing safeguards or safety mitigations |
| Deepseek | ✓ | Unclear* | ✓ | Much broader** |

*Prohibits using Deepseek for purposes resulting in "harmful impacts on physical health, psychology, society, or the economy, or violate scientific and technological ethics." Does not specify self-harm, however.

**Prohibits stealing DeepSeek network data, including reverse engineering to obtain access to data; and "engaging in other activities that endanger the Services' systems, networks, models, and other components," among others.

Figure 7: High-Level Summary of OpenAI's Use Policy

| Company | Service Usage Policies (Rules that apply to users of the services) | | | |
|---|---|---|---|---|
| | Comply with applicable laws (i.e. privacy, prohibited illegal activities) | Prohibited from using services to harm yourself or others | Prohibited from using output from services to harm others (i.e., using output to scam, defraud, bully) | Prohibited from circumventing safeguards or safety mitigations |
| OpenAI | ✓ | ✓ | ✓ | ✓ |

| Company | Service Usage Policies (Rules that apply to users of the services) | | | |
|---|---|---|---|---|
| | Comply with applicable laws (more expansive & includes regulations, regulatory policies, legitimate rights and interests of third parties) | Prohibited from using services to harm yourself or others | Prohibited from using output from services to harm others (i.e., using output to scam, defraud, bully) | Prohibited from circumventing safeguards or safety mitigations |
| Deepseek | ✓ | Unclear* | ✓ | Much broader** |

*Prohibits using Deepseek for purposes resulting in "harmful impacts on physical health, psychology, society, or the economy, or violate scientific and technological ethics." Does not specify self-harm, however.

**Prohibits stealing DeepSeek network data, including reverse engineering to obtain access to data; and "engaging in other activities that endanger the Services' systems, networks, models, and other components," among others.

Figure 8: High-Level Summary of Some Core Components of DeepSeek's Use Policy

> **contractors]** are prohibited from using AI with the intent or purpose to . . . . [u]nlawfully disadvantage an individual based on their ethnicity, national origin, race, sex, gender, gender identity, sexual orientation, disability status, or religion . . . . "[161]

For AI use restrictions, it may be necessary to reference the EU AI Act, which took effect August 1, 2024, and/or California, Colorado, and Utah, which have AI-specific state laws that apply to the private sector.[162]

IX. Roles and responsibilities
Describe the roles and responsibilities required to implement safe and secure AI technologies within an entity. For example, the legal department's role, in part, is to perform due diligence on acquisition contracts for AI products and services before introducing them in the network environment. An example, "Roles and Responsibilities Matrix for Private Entity," provided below gives an overview of some, but not all, roles that may be found within an entity and the corresponding AI-related responsibilities for each of the roles. Not all entities will have every one of these roles. However, many entities need a multidisciplinary cross-section of talent to implement an AI governance and risk management program.

161. The White House, "Framework to Advance AI Governance and Risk Management in National Security," p. 2, Oct. 2024, https://ai.gov/wp-content/uploads/2024/10/NSM-Framework-to-Advance-AI-Governance-and-Risk-Management-in-National-Security.pdf (last visited February 26, 2025).

162. *See* International Association of Privacy Professionals, "State AI Governance Law Chart," February 24, 2025, https://iapp.org/resources/article/us-state-ai-governance-legislation-tracker/#state-ai-governance-law-chart. This tracker focuses on cross-sectoral AI governance bills that apply to private-sector organizations.

## Example Roles and Responsibilities Matrix for Private Entity

| Role | Responsibilities |
|---|---|
| Board of Directors | Approves high-level strategy regarding AI governance and risk management, including such initiatives as financial commitments to AI-related talent, technologies, organic investments, and external acquisition targets, if any. Understands the business operational risks associated with AI investments in the short and long term. Ensures AI initiative and investments align with principles, goals, and objectives. |
| Chief Executive Officer | Sets AI guiding principles and AI strategy, including objectives of AI governance and risk management program, as well as investment levels in talent and technologies. Incorporates advice from general counsel, chief risk officer, and other executives to ensure a comprehensive, strategic approach to AI investments and risk management. |
| General Counsel | Identifies legal and regulatory compliance issues. Evaluates risk exposure and mitigation measures. Evaluates contracts for AI technologies/services to identify potential exposure to risk. Collaborates with colleagues and industry experts to keep abreast of emerging issues and advises CEO and board of directors. |
| Chief Risk Officer | Collaborates with general counsel. Advises the CEO and board of directors on risk mitigation, transference, and/or avoidance measures (e.g., insurance products to reduce AI-related risk). "Develop[s] operational risk management and mitigation processes to prevent losses caused by insufficient or failed procedures, systems or policies."[163] Develops AI incident response plan, including accompanying policies and procedures. Collaborates with general counsel to manage regulatory compliance data. |

163. Dan Byrne, "What Is a Chief Risk Officer (CRO)?," The Corporate Governance Institute, https://www.thecorporategovernanceinstitute.com/insights/lexicon/what-is-a-chief-risk-officer-cro/?srsltid=AfmBOopvL3-ypoN2xk7rkHnLs-k96mj_Yw5ZTQ1xa91DRRqLumquHKnR (last visited March 2, 2025).

| Role | Responsibilities |
|---|---|
| Chief Information Technology Officer/Chief Technology Officer | Collaborates with the chief information officer (CIO) to develop AI risk management program. Understands the current and future information technology assets at strategic and tactical levels, including emerging trends such as AI and associated risks and benefits. Develops IT and AI-related policies and procedures in collaboration with the general counsel and CIO, as appropriate. Advises CEO regarding AI-related technology requests, concerns, and risks. Collaborates as needed on AI training requirements, talent acquisition requests, annual budgets, and immediate issues (e.g., investigations into AI tool–related issues). Identifies and implements technology standards and protocols to keep the network environment safe and accessible. |
| Chief Information Officer | Collaborates with chief information technology officer/chief technology officer to develop AI risk management program. Identifies and applies appropriate information security standards following the industry's best practices and legal and regulatory requirements. Develops and implements information security and AI-specific policies and practices, including AI-related information security training content. Ensures information is safe and secure via technologies (e.g., data loss prevention, endpoint security), data management strategy and program, AI risk governance and risk management program, and accompanying financial and talent requirements to support these and other responsibilities. |

| Role | Responsibilities |
|---|---|
| Human Resources Officer | Budgets and plans for AI-related talent requests from the CEO, chief information technology officer/chief technology officer, CIO, general counsel, and senior management. Leads AI training programs with input from the general counsel, chief information technology officer/chief technology officer, CIO, and others as appropriate. Ensures AI acceptable use policy documents are signed and stored appropriately. Tracks other AI-related employer/employee, contractor, or third-party vendor documentation to ensure files are kept current for internal audit purposes or future compliance and/or audit requests. |
| Senior Management | Oversees the implementation of the AI governance and risk management program, including establishing processes and procedures, hiring talent, managing budgets, and ensuring workforce training on vetted and approved AI tools. Monitors implementation, identifies issues, and reports progress to executives. Submits requests to executives for changes to policies, procedures, and budgets and technology acquisitions. |
| Management | Implements the AI governance and risk management program, executing tasks in accordance with the strategy. Ensures talent delivers tasks on schedule and reports AI issues to senior management. Executes within the budget provided and manages talent across tasks. Ensures AI training of front-line workers is complete and all AI-related documents are signed and delivered to the legal department/human resources or another appropriate department. Monitors front-line workers' use of AI technologies to ensure policies are followed and reports violations to senior management. Conveys requests for AI technologies, talent, changes to policies, changes to procedures, and training to senior management. |

| Role | Responsibilities |
| --- | --- |
| Front-Line Workers | Implement AI governance and risk management tasks. Report issues to management. Use AI technologies as appropriate and in accordance with training. Provide feedback on any AI-related incidents. Request resources to execute AI-related governance and risk management tasks as necessary. |

X. Voluntary commitments
List any commitment documents the entity signed or endorsed. Include a link to those documents for reference. For example, Anthropic voluntary commitments include the White House Voluntary Commitments for Safe, Secure, and Trustworthy AI (2023), the AI Seoul Summit's Frontier AI Safety Commitments (2023), and the Munich AI Elections Accord (2024), among others.[164]

XI. Appendices
a. Acronyms—define acronyms used in the document.
b. AI Acceptable Use Policy Template
c. Glossary—define terms used throughout the document. Use definitions from objective, credible sources such as the Organisation for Economic Co-operation and Development (OECD), the National Institute of Standards and Technology (NIST), the International Organization for Standardization (ISO), and the Massachusetts Institute of Technology (MIT) Technology Review, among others.
d. Document change history—record changes made to the final document. Changes are typically included in a table. Record the date of the change, the department making the change, the type of change (technical, administrative, legal, operational, other), a summary of the change, and the location of the change in the

164. "Anthropic's Transparency Hub: Voluntary Commitments," https://www.anthropic.com/transparency/voluntary-commitments (last visited June 4, 2025).

document. A table and example are provided next for reference.

| Date | Department | Type of Change (technical, administrative, legal, operational, other) | Summary of Change | Location of Change |
|---|---|---|---|---|
| 3/2/2026 | Legal | Legal | New regulatory requirement for AI governance | IV. AI Governance |
| | | | | |
| | | | | |
| | | | | |
| | | | | |

e. References—list the books, articles, laws, regulations, rules, policies, and other materials used to draft the policy.

# APPENDIX B

## Artificial Intelligence (AI) Acceptable Use Policy Template[165]

This template may be modified and used by general counsels, business consultants, information and security professionals, and others to help manage AI-related risks and detail the roles and responsibilities required to implement safe and secure AI technologies. This template is not generated using AI tools/ technologies. It results from numerous months of research and experience. Sources are carefully documented in footnotes.

I. Purpose
What is the purpose of this policy? For example, the purpose of this policy is to clearly articulate the acceptable and unacceptable uses of artificial intelligence (AI) technologies, including AI-enabled or AI-enhanced technologies, in the workplace.

II. Scope
(a) To whom does this policy apply? Employees, contractors, third-party vendors, others?
(b) Are there any to whom this policy does not apply?
(c) What is included in the scope of AI technologies? Examples include, but are not limited to, "machine

165. Template references the LexisNexis Corporation's "Artificial Intelligence (AI) Driven Tools in the Workplace Policy," https://www.lexisnexis.com/pdf/practical-gu (last visited March 1, 2025).

learning, natural language processing, computer vision," conversational chatbots, deep learning platforms, virtual agents, speech recognition, and decision management.[166]

III. Definitions
First, if applicable, reference definitions from international, U.S. federal, and/or state laws. For example, California, Colorado, and Utah have AI-specific state laws applicable to the private sector.[167] Second, draw upon government and quasi-governmental organizations such as the U.S. Department of Commerce, the National Institute of Standards and Technology (NIST), the Organisation for Economic Co-operation and Development (OECD), and the United Nations. Third, consider drawing from academic institutions such as the Massachusetts Institute of Technology (MIT), Stanford University, Dartmouth College, and the California Institute of Technology (CalTech), among others.

IV. Training
(a) Who must take acceptable use policy training? Employees, contractors, third-party vendors, others? Those who fall within scope should be required to take the training.
(b) What will be included in the training? For example, an overview of the general principles; acceptable and unacceptable uses of AI technologies; data handling responsibilities for confidential, sensitive, and proprietary data; incident reporting procedures; and possible consequences for violating this policy.

166. John Terra, "Today's Top 10 AI Technologies: Here's Everything You Should Know," California Institute of Technology, Center for Technology & Management Education, CalTech Bootcamp Blog, November 25, 2024, https://pg-p.ctme.caltech.edu/blog/ai-ml/what-are-todays-top-ten-ai-technologies.

167. *See* International Association of Privacy Professionals, "State AI Governance Law Chart," February 24, 2025, https://iapp.org/resources/article/us-state-ai-governance-legislation-tracker/#state-ai-governance-law-chart. This tracker focuses on cross-sectoral AI governance bills that apply to private-sector organizations.

(c) How will success be determined (e.g., passing tests, earning certificates, etc.)?
(d) How will failure be determined?
(e) How often will training be provided (e.g., biannually, annually, etc.)?
(f) Who will provide the training (e.g., internally sourced, externally sourced, blend of both)?

V. General Principles
(a) When does this policy apply? When using personal devices? Only when using entity-issued devices? When connected to an entity's corporate network regardless of the device being used?
(b) Where are AI technologies typically used, and for what purpose? For example, do legal professionals use an AI tool to assist with drafting legal memorandums and reviewing contracts?
(c) How should practices change to accommodate AI technology integration into job-related responsibilities? AI technologies may produce erroneous outcomes. If AI technologies are used for job-related responsibilities, humans must remain "in the loop" to review content created, recommendations, inferences, and other AI-generated outputs. This review is essential to ensure equity, accuracy, and trust in AI-generated outputs.
(d) Who or what department is responsible for responding if a problem with AI technologies arises? If a problem arises, contact a manager/supervisor/other appropriate individual or department **[include appropriate names, departments]** by phone, instant message, text, or email immediately upon becoming aware of the problem (see section VIII, "Reporting Procedures," for additional details).

VI. Use of Approved AI Technologies
(a) It is best practice to limit use of AI technologies to work and job-related responsibilities and to prohibit personal use.

(b) Does the entity maintain a white list of AI technologies? A white list is a risk management practice whereby only vetted, approved AI technologies are permitted to be downloaded and used (e.g., ChatGPT-4 might be on the white list, but not ChatGPT-3.5).
(c) What is the process used to include new AI technologies on the white list?
(d) How will access control to the white list be managed? What is the process for requesting access to a white-listed technology? What data are collected from the requestor? For example, name, role, department, employee identification number (or equivalent if not an employee), and business reasons for requesting the technology may be collected. This process enables traceability for audit and other appropriate purposes.
(e) What uses of AI technology are restricted? For example, "Refrain from using AI in any manner that violates domestic or international laws . . . . Do not use AI in a manner or for purposes that pose unacceptable levels of risk. Consistent with these goals, . . . **[employees/contractors]** are prohibited from using AI with the intent or purpose to . . . [u]nlawfully disadvantage an individual based on their ethnicity, national origin, race, sex, gender, gender identity, sexual orientation, disability status, or religion . . . ."[168]

VII. Confidential Data
Data classified as "confidential," "sensitive," or "proprietary" (e.g., Social Security numbers, medical records, trade secrets) should not be input into AI technologies. Confidential data are protected "so that unauthorized parties cannot view the data."[169] Sensitive data describes

168. The White House, "Framework to Advance AI Governance and Risk Management in National Security," p. 2, Oct. 2024, https://ai.gov/wp-content/uploads/2024/10/NSM-Framework-to-Advance-AI-Governance-and-Risk-Management-in-National-Security.pdf (last visited February 26, 2025).

169. The National Institute of Standards and Technology (NIST), Computer Security Resource Center, "Confidentiality," https://csrc.nist.gov/glossary/term/confidentiality (last visited March 2, 2025).

data that if lost, misused, accessed, or modified without authorization could undermine security.[170] And proprietary data are related "to or associated with a company's products, business, or activities, including but not limited to financial information; data or statements; trade secrets; product research and development; existing and future product designs and performance specifications; marketing plans or techniques; schematics; client lists; computer programs; processes; and know-how . . . [and the] information must have been developed by the company and not be available to the Government or to the public without restriction from another source."[171]

Data protection and security risks may arise because if data are input into AI technologies, that data may be used to train underlying AI models, thereby exposing "confidential," "sensitive," or "proprietary" data as public. It is, therefore, important to prohibit employees and contractors from using "confidential," "sensitive," or "proprietary" data as inputs to AI technologies. In addition, risk may arise from information licensed from a third party (e.g., Bloomberg, Congressional Quarterly, LexisNexis). These data would likely be prohibited from being input into AI technologies. It is important to review license agreements to be familiar with data restrictions.

In addition, ensuring there is a human in the loop to review AI-generated output (text, images, videos, etc.) may reduce the risk of violating intellectual property rights. Popular AI conversational chatbots, for example, may generate outputs with copyrighted material. One way to address the risk of possible copyright infringement is to include a disclaimer on AI-generated outputs

170. The National Institute of Standards and Technology (NIST), Computer Security Resource Center, "Sensitive," https://csrc.nist.gov/glossary/term/sensitive (last visited March 2, 2025).

171. The National Institute of Standards and Technology (NIST), Computer Security Resource Center, "Proprietary Information (PROPIN)," https://csrc.nist.gov/glossary/term/proprietary_information (last visited March 2, 2025).

(e.g., "This image was created in whole or in part using a third-party vendor artificial intelligence tool.").

Finally, include language regarding data storage and retention is important. For example, language may include: "All employees/contractors must follow the entity's data storage and retention policies, including those governing 'confidential,' 'sensitive,' or 'proprietary' data."

VIII. Reporting Procedures

(a) What is the reporting procedure if a problem arises? For example, contact a manager/supervisor/other appropriate individual or department **[include appropriate names, departments]** by phone, instant message, text, or email immediately upon becoming aware of the problem.

(b) What are the problems that warrant a rapid response? For example, a violation of this policy, AI system failure, and/or issues with AI technology output, such as biased or violent content or hallucinations.

(c) Are there additional steps that should or should not be taken? For example, is it appropriate to unplug or turn off AI technology?

(d) Who should be notified of the problem, should notification be given in writing, what should be included in the notice, and in what timeframe should the notice be given?

(e) When should an investigation be conducted? Who should conduct the investigation?

IX. Violations

Violators of this policy may face disciplinary action up to and including termination of employment or contract.

Questions regarding this policy? Contact: **[individual or department name]**.

X. Changes to Policy

Changes to this policy may be initiated by the chief executive officer (CEO), designee of the CEO, the general counsel, or designee of the general counsel. This policy shall be reviewed and updated periodically, as the AI legal, regulatory, and policy landscape evolves.

**ACKNOWLEDGMENT**

I acknowledge I have read and understand the Artificial Intelligence (AI) Acceptable Use Policy provided by ______________________ **[insert legal name of company]**.

I understand this policy and will abide by it. I understand violations of this policy may result in disciplinary action, up to and including termination of employment or contract (as in the case of an independent contractor or third party).

I understand this policy does not change my status as an at-will employee, independent contractor, or third-party vendor with **[insert legal name of company]**.

For questions about this policy, contact: **[insert appropriate individual or department name and email address]**

| Name of individual or department | |
|---|---|
| Email address | |

**Signature** ___________________________ **Date** ________________

**Printed Name**

_____________________________________

**Effective Date:**

_____________________________________

# APPENDIX C

## Ten Steps to Develop an AI Policy

Adapted from Accountancy Ireland, the following are ten steps to develop an AI policy for an organization. Created in 2023, this process is clear and stands the test of time. The process applies to nearly any organization and calls for members of the board of directors to take the lead in AI policy development. If a board of directors does not apply to your organization, consider other leaders such as the chief executive officer, general counsel, chief risk officer, chief information officer, chief technology officer, human resources officer, and so on.

Some organizations create a dedicated AI policy committee of leaders, such as those previously mentioned, and/or the designees of those leaders. While not every organization will have each of these roles, the AI policy should be drafted by a multidisciplinary team of professionals equipped to make strategic-level decisions considering the organization's risk appetite, financial health, talent pool, legal liability, information technology and security assets and vulnerabilities, information and cybersecurity risk, and overall operating environment.

| Ten Steps to Develop an AI Policy[172] | |
|---|---|
| 1 | Establish working group—Business leaders/board members form group to lead AI policy effort |
| 2 | Educate members—Understand AI concepts, ethics, economic impact, liability, security, and so on |
| 3 | Define policy objectives—Why adopt AI (e.g., increase efficiency/productivity) |
| 4 | Develop ethical principles—Ethical principles guide AI policy (e.g., transparency, fairness, etc.) |
| 5 | Understand legal landscape—Identify and understand the state, federal and applicable international laws and regulations |
| 6 | Identify use cases and risk—Where will AI be used, for what purpose, by whom? What are the risks associated with each use case? |
| 7 | Establish governance and accountability—Roles and responsibilities for AI governance |
| 8 | Ensure transparency—Require clear explanation of algorithms and data practices |
| 9 | Ensure continuous monitoring and evaluation—Develop mechanisms to monitor systems and evaluate AI policy efficacy |
| 10 | Communicate AI policy—Language should be clear and include implementation guidance |

172. Stephen Conmy, "Ten Steps to Hhelp Your Board Establish an AI Policy," Accountancy Ireland, May 26, 2023, https://www.charteredaccountants.ie/Accountancy-Ireland/Articles2/News/Latest-News/ten-steps-to-help-your-board-establish-an-ai-policy.

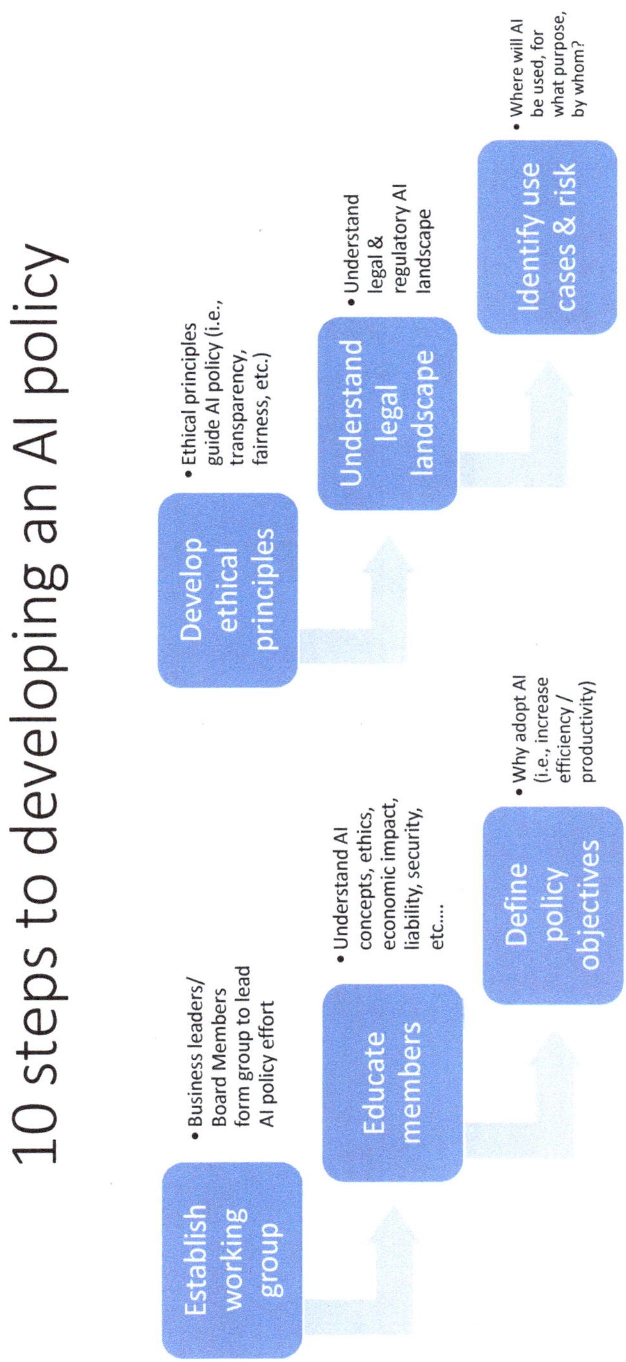
10 steps to developing an AI policy
Establish working group
• Business leaders/ Board Members form group to lead AI policy effort
Educate members
• Understand AI concepts, ethics, economic impact, liability, security, etc....
Define policy objectives
• Why adopt AI (i.e., increase efficiency / productivity)
Develop ethical principles
• Ethical principles guide AI policy (i.e., transparency, fairness, etc.)
Understand legal landscape
• Understand legal & regulatory AI landscape
Identify use cases & risk
• Where will AI be used, for what purpose, by whom?

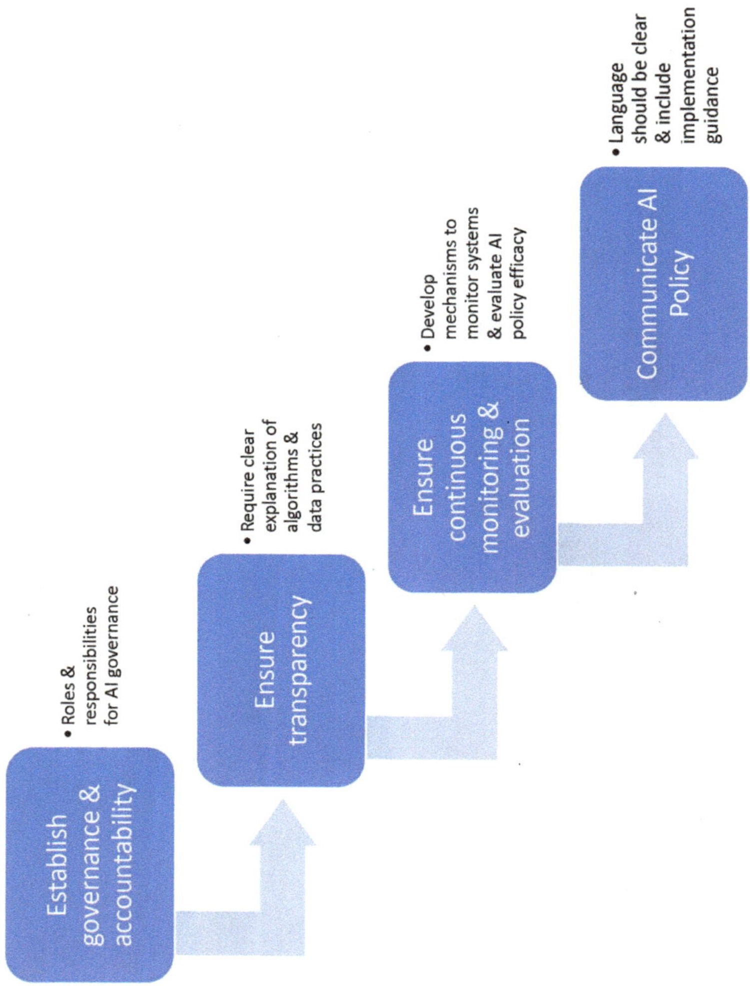


Source: Stephen Conmy, "Ten Steps to Help Your Board Establish an AI Policy," Accountancy Ireland, May 26, 2023, https://www.charteredaccountants.ie/Accountancy-Ireland/Articles2/News/Latest-News/ten-steps-to-help-your-board-establish-an-ai-policy.

# APPENDIX D

## AI Policy Template

This template may be modified and used by general counsels, business consultants, information and security professionals, and others to help manage AI-related risks and detail the roles and responsibilities required to implement safe and secure AI technologies.

I. Purpose

What is the purpose of this document?

Generally, the AI policy outlines how artificial intelligence (AI) is safely and responsibly acquired, deployed, monitored, and decommissioned within an operating environment such as a private business, government organization, or academic institution.

II. Scope

To whom does this policy apply? Who may be excluded from it?

Generally, everyone working as an employee or a contractor must be aware of, read, understand, and follow the AI policy. Furthermore, it is best practice for the employee/contractor to sign and date a written statement acknowledging that they have read, understand, and will follow the AI policy.

III. AI Systems
What AI systems will be purchased, developed, contracted for, or used in the operating environment? Identify all AI technologies, including applications and services, and assess the accompanying risk for each. Are there any AI systems, vendors, or service providers that are prohibited or restricted (e.g., products and services produced directly or indirectly by Huawei Technologies Co., Ltd., a Chinese multinational corporation and technology company)?

IV. Definitions
Provide definitions of AI terms. Some example terms are provided for reference.

| Term | Definition | Source |
| --- | --- | --- |
| Accountability | "Presupposes transparency . . . [which] reflects the extent to which information about an AI system and its outputs is available to individuals interacting with such a system—regardless of whether they are even aware that they are doing so. Meaningful transparency provides access to appropriate levels of information based on the stage of the AI lifecycle and tailored to the role or knowledge of AI actors or individuals interacting with or using the AI system. By promoting higher levels of understanding, transparency increases confidence in the AI system." | National Institute of Standards and Technology (NIST), Trustworthy & Responsible AI Resource Center, "3 AI Risks and Trustworthiness," https://airc.nist.gov/airmf-resources/airmf/3-sec-characteristics/ (last visited March 28, 2025). |

| Term | Definition | Source |
|---|---|---|
| Artificial intelligence (AI) | "A machine-based system that can, for a given set of human-defined objectives, make predictions, recommendations, or decisions influencing real or virtual environments." | Section 5002 of the National Defense Authorization Act for Fiscal Year 2021 (P.L. 116-283)[173] |
| AI systems | "AI is a catchall term for a set of technologies that make computers do things that are thought to require intelligence when done by people." | Will Douglas Heaven, "What Is AI?," *MIT Technology Review*, July 10, 2024, https://www.technologyreview.com/2024/07/10/1094475/what-is-artificial-intelligence-ai-definitive-guide/. |
| | "Outputs such as content, predictions, recommendations, or decisions influencing the environments [AI models] interact with." | Article 3(1), European Union (EU) AI Act (2024)[174] |
| | "AI systems use machine and human-based inputs to—(A) perceive real and virtual environments; (B) abstract such perceptions into models through analysis in an automated manner; and (C) use model inference to formulate options for information or action." | Section 5002 of the National Defense Authorization Act for Fiscal Year 2021 (P.L. 116-283) |
| Algorithm | A procedure used to solve a problem in a finite number of steps; encoded procedures that transform input data into a defined output based on specific calculations. | Woodrow Barfield & Ugo Pagallo, *Research Handbook on the Law of Artificial Intelligence* 4 (2022). |

173. William M. (Mac) Thornberry National Defense Authorization Act for Fiscal Year 2021 (NDAA FY21), Pub. L. No. 116-283, § 5002, 134 Stat. 3388 (2021).

174. EU Artificial Intelligence Act, Article 3: Definitions, February 2, 2025, https://artificialintelligenceact.eu/article/3/.

| Term | Definition | Source |
|---|---|---|
| Explainability | The rationale for how an AI model decision/recommendation/outcome was reached, including a description of contributing factors. Explanations are important for legal/regulatory compliance in many cases and meeting end-user expectations for transparency of AI. For example, many, if not all, U.S. credit scoring firms use AI-enabled technologies to calculate individual credit scores. These firms should disclose to the end user—the individual—how the AI-enabled credit score was calculated. | IBM, "What is Explainable AI?" March 29, 2023, https://www.ibm.com/think/topics/explainable-ai |
| Fairness | Fairness refers to AI models producing unbiased recommendations, decisions, and predictions to avoid the risk of "potential legal, financial, and reputational damage." | IBM, "Fairness," December 6, 2022, https://www.ibm.com/design/ai/ethics/fairness/ |
| | An attribute of an AI system that prioritizes relatively equal treatment of individuals or groups in its decisions and actions in a constant, accurate manner. | IAPP, "Key Terms for AI Governance," July 2024, https://iapp.org/resources/article/key-terms-for-ai-governance/ (last visited March 31, 2025). |
| Generalization | The ability of an ML model to understand the underlying patterns and trends in its training data and apply what it has learned to make predictions or decisions about new, unseen data. | IAPP, "Key Terms for AI Governance," July 2024, https://iapp.org/resources/article/key-terms-for-ai-governance/ (last visited March 31, 2025). |

| Term | Definition | Source |
|---|---|---|
| Human rights | "Rights inherent to all human beings . . . [including] the right to life and liberty, freedom from slavery and torture, freedom of opinion and expression, the right to work and education, and many more. Everyone is entitled to these rights, without discrimination." | United Nations, Global Compact, "Artificial Intelligence and Human Rights," 2024, https://unglobalcompact.org/library/6206. |
| Model | "A model . . . is nothing more than an abstract representation of some process, be it a baseball game, an oil company's supply chain, a foreign government's actions, or a movie theater's attendance." | Cathy O'Neil, *Weapons of Math Destruction* 18 (2016). |
| Privacy | "AI privacy is the practice of protecting personal or sensitive information collected, used, shared, or stored by AI." | Alice Gomstyn & Alexandra Jonker, "Exploring Privacy Issues in the Age of AI," IBM, September 30, 2024, https://www.ibm.com/think/insights/ai-privacy. |
| Robustness | The "ability of a system to maintain its level of performance under a variety of circumstances . . . . Robustness requires not only that the system perform exactly as it does under expected uses, but also that it should perform in ways that minimize potential harms to people if operating in an unexpected setting." | National Institute of Standards and Technology (NIST), Trustworthy & Responsible AI Resource Center, "3 AI Risks and Trustworthiness," https://airc.nist.gov/airmf-resources/airmf/3-sec-characteristics/ (last visited March 28, 2025). |

| Term | Definition | Source |
|---|---|---|
| Safety | AI systems should "not under defined conditions" endanger "human life, health, property, or the environment . . . ." Safe AI systems use "responsible design, development, and deployment practices; clear information to deployers on responsible use of the system; responsible decision-making by deployers and end users; and explanations and documentation of risks based on empirical evidence of incidents." | National Institute of Standards and Technology (NIST), Trustworthy & Responsible AI Resource Center, "3 AI Risks and Trustworthiness," https://airc.nist.gov/airmf-resources/airmf/3-sec-characteristics/ (last visited March 28, 2025). |
| Security | AI systems should be secure and include "protocols to avoid, protect against, respond to, or recover from attacks." Security encompasses resilience, which "relates to robustness and goes beyond the provenance of the data to encompass unexpected or adversarial use (or abuse or misuse) of the model or data." | National Institute of Standards and Technology (NIST), Trustworthy & Responsible AI Resource Center, "3 AI Risks and Trustworthiness," https://airc.nist.gov/airmf-resources/airmf/3-sec-characteristics/ (last visited March 28, 2025). |
| Societal impacts | Assessing the societal impacts of AI is important to determine whether or not to adopt and use AI technologies within an organization or environment. Labor disruption and/or displacement are real societal consequences of adopting AI. What might job losses mean for a community? | Neelanjana Gautam, "Unraveling the Social Impacts of Artificial Intelligence," IC Davis Office of Research, University of California, August 7, 2024, https://research.ucdavis.edu/unraveling-the-social-impacts-of-artificial-intelligence/. |

| Term | Definition | Source |
|---|---|---|
| Sustainable development | The ability to tap into and harness compute power for AI and "the ability of emerging countries to leverage technological developments" are key to accelerating their sustainable development goals. "Compute power is fast becoming the new and the next facet of the digital divide." | United Nations Development Programme, "AI for Sustainable Development," May 9, 2024, https://www.undp.org/digital/blog/ai-sustainable-development. |
| Transparency | Refers to how a model was created, including the data used to train the model and the process used to develop a recommendation, decision, or prediction. "AI transparency goes beyond just explaining AI decision-making processes. It encompasses factors related to the development of AI systems and their deployment, such as the AI training data and who has access to it." | Alexandra Jonker, Amanda McGrath & Alice Gomstyn, "What Is AI Transparency?," IBM, September 6, 2024, https://www.ibm.com/think/topics/ai-transparency. |

V. Objectives

What are the organization's goals in adopting AI technology? Generally, AI is adopted to expedite processes, improve worker productivity, decrease labor cost, promote research and development (innovation), and/or enhance customer service experience. For example, OpenAI's safety objectives, as of 2023, include:[175]

- Build increasingly safe AI systems

175. OpenAI, "Our Approach to AI Safety," April 5, 2023, https://openai.com/index/our-approach-to-ai-safety/ (last visited March 28, 2025).

- Learn from real-world use to improve safeguards
- Protect children
- Protect privacy
- Improve factual accuracy
- Continue research and engagement

### Identify Potential AI Use Cases and Associated Risks

It is best practice to explain use cases or applications of AI within the organization. Where will AI be used, by whom, and for what purpose? Explain the associated risks (e.g., hallucinations, bias, errors, etc.) and any mitigation measures to manage these risks.

VI. AI Principles

What are the foundational AI principles? Principles are foundational to developing an AI policy and are the first step in establishing AI governance. It may be helpful to reference the Organisation for Economic Co-operation and Development (OECD) list of five AI principles published in 2019 and updated in May 2024. The five OECD AI principles are:

i. Accountability
ii. Robustness, security, and safety
iii. Transparency and explainability
iv. Human rights and democratic values, including fairness and privacy
v. Inclusive growth, sustainable development, and well-being

The European Union, the United States, and the U.K. have endorsed these OECD AI principles.[176] For example, though some terms differ, the Microsoft Corporation's six AI principles align with the OECD's AI principles.[177]

176. OECD, "OECD AI Principles Overview," https://oecd.ai/en/ai-principles (last visited March 26, 2025).

177. https://www.microsoft.com/en/ai/principles-and-approach.

| Microsoft's AI Principles | |
|---|---|
| Fairness | Inclusiveness |
| Reliability[178] and safety | Transparency |
| Privacy and security | Accountability |

VII. Roles and Responsibilities

What roles and departments/divisions are responsible for executing the AI policy objectives and for the development, deployment, and monitoring of AI? Clearly describe who is responsible for what activities/functions, accountability to ensure compliance, and AI risk management measures throughout the AI life cycle.[179]

Who are the primary contacts responsible for developing the AI policy? Generally, a multidisciplinary team develops the AI policy. For example, senior contacts within the legal/regulatory department, acquisitions/supply chain management, executive management, information security and information technology, and risk management coordinate to develop an AI policy within an organization.

How often is the AI policy updated? It is best practice to review and update the AI policy at least once a year and/or upon making substantive changes/updates to the operating environment, such as introducing new/updated AI technologies.

VIII. Legal and Regulatory Compliance

Foundational to developing the AI policy, much like selecting and articulating the AI principles, is establishing the scope of legal and regulatory compliance. Which

178. Reliability is an attribute of an AI system that ensures it behaves as expected and performs its intended function consistently and accurately, even with new data that it has not been trained on. IAPP, "Key Terms for AI Governance," July 2024, https://iapp.org/resources/article/key-terms-for-ai-governance/ (last visited March 31, 2025).

179. Dan Byrne, "Ten Steps to Creating an AI Policy," Corporate Governance Institute, 2024, https://www.thecorporategovernanceinstitute.com/insights/guides/creating-an-ai-policy/?srsltid=AfmBOoo8VSzdAJxEkWSxvOVU-y2kUQKUpFYm0hmQgI_UwP1iWeYnk4_9.

domestic and international laws and regulations on AI, data protection, data privacy, cybersecurity, other information security, and information technology apply? Do industry-specific guidelines or best practices apply? What legal and/or regulatory risks are avoided/mitigated/managed via this policy?[180]

IX. Contacts
Who does the employees/contractors contact if they have questions regarding this policy? Typically, the human resources department/division or the legal department/division is listed as the initial point of contact.

**Department:**
**Phone:**
**Email:**

**Signature** ______________________________ **Date** ______________

**Printed Name**

________________________________________

**Effective Date**

________________________________________

180. *Id.*

# APPENDIX E

## Glossary of Terms

| Term | Definition | Source |
|---|---|---|
| Accountability | "Presupposes transparency . . . [which] reflects the extent to which information about an AI system and its outputs is available to individuals interacting with such a system—regardless of whether they are even aware that they are doing so. Meaningful transparency provides access to appropriate levels of information based on the stage of the AI lifecycle and tailored to the role or knowledge of AI actors or individuals interacting with or using the AI system. By promoting higher levels of understanding, transparency increases confidence in the AI system." | National Institute of Standards and Technology (NIST), Trustworthy & Responsible AI Resource Center, "3 AI Risks and Trustworthiness," https://airc.nist.gov/airmf-resources/airmf/3-sec-characteristics/ (last visited March 28, 2025). |
| | Accountability ensures that an AI system's actions, decisions, and outcomes can be traced back to the entity responsible for them. | IAPP, "Key Terms for AI Governance," July 2024, https://iapp.org/resources/article/key-terms-for-ai-governance/ (last visited March 31, 2025). |

| Term | Definition | Source |
|---|---|---|
| Algorithm | A procedure used to solve a problem in a finite number of steps; encoded procedures that transform input data into a defined output based on specific calculations. | Woodrow Barfield & Ugo Pagallo, *Research Handbook on the Law of Artificial Intelligence* 4 (2022). |
| Artificial general intelligence (AGI) | AI that is considered to have human-level intelligence and strong generalization capability to achieve goals and carry out a variety of tasks in different contexts and environments. AGI remains a theoretical field of research. | IAPP, "Key Terms for AI Governance," July 2024, https://iapp.org/resources/article/key-terms-for-ai-governance/ (last visited March 31, 2025). |
| Artificial intelligence (AI) | "A machine-based system that can, for a given set of human-defined objectives, make predictions, recommendations, or decisions influencing real or virtual environments." | Section 5002 of the National Defense Authorization Act for Fiscal Year 2021 (P.L. 116-283)[181] |
| | "Outputs such as content, predictions, recommendations, or decisions influencing the environments [AI models] interact with." | Article 3(1), European Union (EU) AI Act (2024)[182] |
| | "AI is a catchall term for a set of technologies that make computers do things that are thought to require intelligence when done by people." | Will Douglas Heaven, "What Is AI?," *MIT Technology Review*, July 10, 2024, https://www.technologyreview.com/2024/07/10/1094475/what-is-artificial-intelligence-ai-definitive-guide/. |
| AI governance | A system of laws, policies, frameworks, practices, and processes at international, national, and organizational levels. It helps to manage AI technology and associated risks. | IAPP, "Key Terms for AI Governance," July 2024, https://iapp.org/resources/article/key-terms-for-ai-governance/ (last visited March 31, 2025). |

181. William M. (Mac) Thornberry National Defense Authorization Act for Fiscal Year 2021 (NDAA FY21), Pub. L. No. 116-283, § 5002, 134 Stat. 3388 (2021).

182. EU Artificial Intelligence Act, Article 3: Definitions, February 2, 2025, https://artificialintelligenceact.eu/article/3/.

| Term | Definition | Source |
|---|---|---|
| AI systems | "AI systems use machine and human-based inputs to—(A) perceive real and virtual environments; (B) abstract such perceptions into models through analysis in an automated manner; and (C) use model inference to formulate options for information or action." | Section 5002 of the National Defense Authorization Act for Fiscal Year 2021 (P.L. 116-283) |
| Automated decision-making | The process of making a decision by technological means without human involvement, either in whole or in part. | IAPP, "Key Terms for AI Governance," July 2024, https://iapp.org/resources/article/key-terms-for-ai-governance/ (last visited March 31, 2025). |
| Bias | There are several types of bias within AI. Computational bias is a systematic error of deviation from the true value of a prediction that originates from a model's assumptions or the input data itself. Cognitive bias refers to inaccurate individual judgment or distorted thinking. Societal bias leads to systematic prejudice, favoritism, and/or discrimination in favor of or against an individual or group. Bias can impact AI model outcomes and pose a risk to individual rights and liberties. | IAPP, "Key Terms for AI Governance," July 2024, https://iapp.org/resources/article/key-terms-for-ai-governance/ (last visited March 31, 2025). |
| Computer vision | A field of AI that enables computers to process and analyze images, videos, and other visual inputs. | IAPP, "Key Terms for AI Governance," July 2024, https://iapp.org/resources/article/key-terms-for-ai-governance/ (last visited March 31, 2025). |

| Term | Definition | Source |
|---|---|---|
| Data governance | "[A] system of decision rights and accountabilities for information-related processes, executed according to agreed-upon models which describe who can take what actions with what information, and when, under what circumstances, using what methods." | The Data Governance Institute, "Definitions of Data Governance," https://datagovernance.com/the-data-governance-basics/definitions-of-data-governance/ (last visited March 31, 2025). |
| Explainability | The rationale for how an AI model decision/recommendation/outcome was reached, including a description of contributing factors. Explanations are important for legal/regulatory compliance in many cases and meeting end-user expectations for transparency of AI. For example, many, if not all, U.S. credit scoring firms use AI-enabled technologies to calculate individual credit scores. These firms should disclose to the end user—the individual—how the AI-enabled credit score was calculated. | Dmitriy Rybalko, "AI Model Lifecycle Management: Monitor Phase," November 20, 2020. |
| Fairness | Fairness refers to AI models producing unbiased recommendations, decisions, and predictions to avoid the risk of "potential legal, financial, and reputational damage." | Dmitriy Rybalko, "AI Model Lifecycle Management: Monitor Phase," November 20, 2020. |
| Generative AI | A field of AI that uses deep learning trained on large data sets to create new content, such as written text, code, images, simulations, and videos. | IAPP, "Key Terms for AI Governance," July 2024, https://iapp.org/resources/article/key-terms-for-ai-governance/ (last visited March 31, 2025). |

| Term | Definition | Source |
|---|---|---|
| Hallucinations | Instances in which generative AI models create seemingly plausible but factually incorrect outputs under the appearance of fact. | IAPP, "Key Terms for AI Governance," July 2024, https://iapp.org/resources/article/key-terms-for-ai-governance/ (last visited March 31, 2025). |
| Human rights | "Rights inherent to all human beings . . . [including] the right to life and liberty, freedom from slavery and torture, freedom of opinion and expression, the right to work and education, and many more. Everyone is entitled to these rights, without discrimination." | United Nations, Global Compact, "Artificial Intelligence and Human Rights," 2024, https://unglobalcompact.org/library/6206. |
| Input data | Data provided to or directly acquired by a learning algorithm or ML model to produce an output. It forms the basis upon which the ML model will learn make predictions, and/or carry out tasks. | IAPP, "Key Terms for AI Governance," July 2024, https://iapp.org/resources/article/key-terms-for-ai-governance/ (last visited March 31, 2025). |
| Large language models (LLMs) | LLMs are a form of ML utilizing deep learning algorithms to create models pretrained on massive text data sets for the purpose of language learning to analyze and learn patterns and relationships among characters, words, and phrases. | IAPP, "Key Terms for AI Governance," July 2024, https://iapp.org/resources/article/key-terms-for-ai-governance/ (last visited March 31, 2025). |
| Machine learning (ML) | A subfield of AI involving algorithms that enable computer systems to iteratively learn from and then make decisions, inferences, or predictions based on input data. | IAPP, "Key Terms for AI Governance," July 2024, https://iapp.org/resources/article/key-terms-for-ai-governance/ (last visited March 31, 2025). |

| Term | Definition | Source |
|---|---|---|
| Model | "A model . . . is nothing more than an abstract representation of some process, be it a baseball game, an oil company's supply chain, a foreign government's actions, or a movie theater's attendance." | Cathy O'Neil, *Weapons of Math Destruction* 18 (2016). |
| Neural networks | A type of model used in ML that mimics the way neurons in the brain interact with multiple processing layers, including at least one hidden layer. | IAPP, "Key Terms for AI Governance," July 2024, https://iapp.org/resources/article/key-terms-for-ai-governance/ (last visited March 31, 2025). |
| Privacy | "AI privacy is the practice of protecting personal or sensitive information collected, used, shared, or stored by AI." | Alice Gomstyn & Alexandra Jonker, "Exploring Privacy Issues in the Age of AI," IBM, September 30, 2024, https://www.ibm.com/think/insights/ai-privacy. |
| Reliability | Reliability is an attribute of an AI system that ensures it behaves as expected and performs its intended function consistently and accurately, even with new data that it has not been trained on. | IAPP, "Key Terms for AI Governance," July 2024, https://iapp.org/resources/article/key-terms-for-ai-governance/ (last visited March 31, 2025). |
| Robustness | The "ability of a system to maintain its level of performance under a variety of circumstances . . . . Robustness requires not only that the system perform exactly as it does under expected uses, but also that it should perform in ways that minimize potential harms to people if operating in an unexpected setting." | National Institute of Standards and Technology (NIST), Trustworthy & Responsible AI Resource Center, "3 AI Risks and Trustworthiness," https://airc.nist.gov/airmf-resources/airmf/3-sec-characteristics/ (last visited March 28, 2025). |

| Term | Definition | Source |
|---|---|---|
| Safety | AI systems should "not under defined conditions" endanger "human life, health, property, or the environment . . . ." Safe AI systems use "responsible design, development, and deployment practices; clear information to deployers on responsible use of the system; responsible decision-making by deployers and end users; and explanations and documentation of risks based on empirical evidence of incidents." | National Institute of Standards and Technology (NIST), Trustworthy & Responsible AI Resource Center, "3 AI Risks and Trustworthiness," https://airc.nist.gov/airmf-resources/airmf/3-sec-characteristics/ (last visited March 28, 2025). |
| Security | AI systems should be secure and include "protocols to avoid, protect against, respond to, or recover from attacks." Security encompasses resilience, which "relates to robustness and goes beyond the provenance of the data to encompass unexpected or adversarial use (or abuse or misuse) of the model or data." | National Institute of Standards and Technology (NIST), Trustworthy & Responsible AI Resource Center, "3 AI Risks and Trustworthiness," https://airc.nist.gov/airmf-resources/airmf/3-sec-characteristics/ (last visited March 28, 2025). |
| Societal impacts | Assessing the societal impacts of AI is important to determine whether or not to adopt and use AI technologies within an organization or environment. Labor disruption and/or displacement are real societal consequences of adopting AI. What might job losses mean for a community? | Neelanjana Gautam, "Unraveling the Social Impacts of Artificial Intelligence," IC Davis Office of Research, University of California, August 7, 2024, https://research.ucdavis.edu/unraveling-the-social-impacts-of-artificial-intelligence/. |

| Term | Definition | Source |
|---|---|---|
| Sustainable development | The ability to tap into and harness compute power for AI and "the ability of emerging countries to leverage technological developments" are key to accelerating their sustainable development goals. "Compute power is fast becoming the new and the next facet of the digital divide." | United Nations Development Programme, "AI for Sustainable Development," May 9, 2024, https://www.undp.org/digital/blog/ai-sustainable-development. |
| Training data | A subset of the data set that is used to train an ML model until it can accurately predict outcomes, find patterns, or identify structures within the training data. | IAPP, "Key Terms for AI Governance," July 2024, https://iapp.org/resources/article/key-terms-for-ai-governance/ (last visited March 31, 2025). |
| Transparency | Refers to how a model was created, including the data used to train the model and the process used to develop a recommendation, decision, or prediction. "AI transparency goes beyond just explaining AI decision-making processes. It encompasses factors related to the development of AI systems and their deployment, such as the AI training data and who has access to it." | Alexandra Jonker, Amanda McGrath & Alice Gomstyn, "What Is AI Transparency?," IBM, September 6, 2024, https://www.ibm.com/think/topics/ai-transparency. |
| Trustworthy AI | Trustworthy AI, responsible AI, and ethical AI are generally used interchangeably to refer to "principle-based AI development and AI governance, including the principles of security, safety, transparency, explainability, accountability, privacy and nondiscrimination/nonbias . . . , among others." | IAPP, "Key Terms for AI Governance," July 2024, https://iapp.org/resources/article/key-terms-for-ai-governance/ (last visited March 31, 2025). |

| Term | Definition | Source |
|---|---|---|
| Variable (also known as features) | A measurable attribute, characteristic, or unit that can take on different values. A variable is a quantity or value that can change. For example, in the formula for risk: risk (r) equals probability (p) times severity (s). Here, the variables are the (p) and (s), which, when multiplied together, result in the (r). It stands to reason that a higher value of either or both of the variables (p) and (s) reflects higher (r). | IAPP, "Key Terms for AI Governance," July 2024, https://iapp.org/resources/article/key-terms-for-ai-governance/ (last visited March 31, 2025). |

# Index